Bloom Where You Are Planted and SHINE!

Compiled By:
Rebecca Hall Gruyter
International Best Selling Author

www.womenterprises.com

COPYRIGHT 2017

ALL RIGHTS RESERVED

NO PART OF THIS PUBLICATION MAY BE REPRODUCED,

STORED IN A RETRIEVAL SYSTEM, OR TRANSMITTED IN ANY FORM

OR BY ANY MEANS, ELECTRONIC, MECHANICAL, PHOTOCOPY,

RECORDING, OR ANY OTHER, WITHOUT THE PRIOR WRITTEN PERMISSION OF THE AUTHORS.

Table of Contents

Foreword 1
About The Compiler 6
Section 1: Overcoming Challenges 7
   Life Is A Constant Construction Zone By Dixie Bennett 8
   Choose Love By Melinda Gulick 18
   Remember Who You Truly Are By Phyllis Flemings ... 27
   Lost, Loss And Learning To Trust Again By Sonya Williams 35
   Let Come, Let Be, Let Go By Ione Wendy Sidwell 42
   Let's Get Tender By Marlene Elizabeth 51
Section 2: Stand In Your Truth 60
   Choose To Bloom By Teresa Hawley Howard 61
   Secrets Worth Telling By Brandy T. Jones 67
   An Olympian's Mindset By Coach Sherry Winn 76
   The Strength Of Your Story By Jeanne Alford 87
   Awaken To Every Moment By Holly Reese, Msom, L.Ac. 96
Section 3: Discover Your Beauty, Gifts, Talents And Abilities 104
   Driven To Thrive By Samantha Jansen 105
   Bloom When Life Falls Apart By Nancy Monson 113
   Live To Love By Fariba Haidari 123
   Unleash…Come Home To You By Mary E. Knippel 132

Grow Your Self Under The Sun By Marlowe Allenbright 142

Section 4: Bloom **151**

Forgiveness Can Bring Out Your Shine! By Carolyn Cj Jones 152

Choosing To Love Again By Jim T. Chong 162

My Blossoming Journe By Catherine M Laub 173

Be Heart-Strong By Deb Dutcher 182

Mirror Mirror By Jon Missall 191

I Am A 'Holy Shifter' By Beverly Brooke Peterson .. 196

Section 5: Shine! **207**

Confidence—The Art Of Being Confident By John F. Hall, Lcdr, Usn(Ret) Mba, Bsee, Mscs 208

My Moscow Adventures By Barbara Gross 217

The World Is Made Of Stories By Caitríona Reed 227

Blossom In The Midst Of The Storm By Trisha Garrett 235

Closing Thoughts **245**

Books Featuring Rebecca Hall Gruyter **247**

Independent Reviews **249**

FOREWORD

"Bloom Where You Are Planted and SHINE!"
Rebecca Hall Gruyter, Book Compiler

Thank you for leaning into Bloom Where You Are Planted and SHINE! I'm honored and excited to bring this powerful book to you, featuring over 25 experts that are committed to helping you SHINE powerfully in your life!

As a women's empowerment leader, I know a lot about being disempowered and how to overcome that in order to step into your passion, power, and gifts so that you SHINE! I celebrate you saying 'yes' to this book and to yourself! It is a courageous act to say 'yes' to you and to be willing to let others walk beside you to support and cheer you on in life.

I was honored when Teresa Hawley-Howard from WOM Enterprises wanted to publish a book for us. WOM leaned in to the heart and vision of bringing multiple heart-centered authors and experts together to share their respective journeys and wisdom, as well as profound and practical tips to empower our readers to Bloom Where You Are Planted and SHINE. In sharing their stories, they will equip and empower you to overcome challenges, stand in your truth, grow your roots deeply, and SHINE!

I believe this book is a living and interactive book that will speak wisdom, encouragement, and power into your life. Your heart will be touched and you will be motivated to take action to step forward powerfully in your life. I want to invite you to pause, take a deep breath, and be ready to receive these powerful stories and messages so they can ignite a fire in you, inspire courage in you, and focus your purpose in your life to encourage you to take action now and SHINE!

I'm passionate about women stepping forward and sharing their wisdom, heart, lives, and stories because I know firsthand what it like to come from a much-disempowered place. I experienced all types of abuse during my most formative years – the tender ages of 5 to 13. I actually continued to visit that abusive environment until the age of eighteen. This environment of abuse made me believe false messages like: "I am not okay," "there is something wrong with me," that it must be "my fault," and "that it is NOT safe to be seen or heard."

As a result, I became an expert in hiding. When I was finally rescued by my birth father and placed in his home with my stepmother, who became the mother of my heart, I was able start my healing journey. On this journey, I discovered that these beliefs I had embraced were actually lies. I discovered that I am beautifully and wonderfully made (just like you), on purpose and for a purpose; that I matter and am needed just as I am; that it wasn't my fault; and ultimately that it is safe to be seen, heard, and SHINE!

So, my mission - the calling of my heart - is to help others understand these same truths: We are all beautifully and wonderfully made and needed just as we are. When we step forward and share the gift of us, it makes a difference in our lives and in the lives of those around us. This means we have to be willing to be seen on the same level that we are wanting to serve and make a difference in the world. **The more you SHINE, the more you are paving the way for others while sharing the amazing gift of you with the world.**

My heart's desire and calling is to equip and empower women to step into the center of their lives - not just living life as a supporting character or a role we can hold in life. I want you to really step forward fully in your life. Bring it all. Authentically and powerfully share your story, life, and heart with others. Some of the greatest gifts I have been given are by women and men who invested their life and heart in me. This book is allowing us the opportunity to pour into you. To support, celebrate, and to encourage you to Bloom Where You Are Planted and SHINE!

We each need others to encourage us, to speak wisdom and truth into us, to love us and cheer us on, and to help us stand up again when we fall. This book will walk beside you to help you run and not grow weary, to complete all that you are called to complete, and to SHINE in your life and business!

In creating this book, I asked each heart-centered and powerful co-author to share some of their personal story and journey with you. As they share from their respective journeys with you, they share what they have learned. They share their wisdom and what they wish someone had encouraged them with or whispered in their ear - especially in those dark and challenging times. They are committed to pouring into you, to equip and empower you in your life.

Throughout the chapters you will feel a consistent and transparent heartbeat to support you in very real ways as the authors often share what they wish they would have known. We want to make your path and journey easier for you to step forward to Bloom Where You Are Planted and SHINE! As the book compiler, I'm so proud of what each co-author has shared in their chapters, and am honored to have each of them leaning in to support you. I am equally honored that you have said "yes" to our book and are entrusting us to support you on your journey.

Now it's your turn. Are you going to lean in and learn from the wisdom within this book? Will you let us walk beside you on your journey of life? We want to lift you up, support you, encourage, and empower you. It is your choice. We want to help you grow deep roots that can weather the storms in life. You can choose to open the pages and let them pour into you, or you can put this book on a shelf. My heart and prayer is that you will say "yes" to you and lean into the powerful messages of hope that are waiting to pour into you, your heart, and your life.

You have unique gifts, talents, abilities, stories, journeys, and perspectives that you alone can bring forward. Those in your life need you, your message, your wisdom, your perspective, gifts, talents, and heart. You are a beautiful flower in the garden of life with your own fragrance, color, style, season, texture, and beauty that only you can bring forward. When we shrink back or hide, the garden becomes less vibrant and we all miss out. Be willing to share the gift of you with those around you and with the world! Be willing to be seen on the same level you are willing/wanting to serve.

Here is how to get the most out of this powerful book. It is divided into five sections, each one designed to meet you exactly where you are and to support you in your journey of Blooming Where You are Planted and SHINE:

"Overcoming Challenges"; "Stand In Your Truth"; "Discover Your Beauty, Gifts, and Talents!"; "Bloom Where You Are Planted"; and "SHINE!" I encourage you to pick the section that pulls at your heart the most each time you pick up the book. Then select one or two chapters in that section to support you with the focus that will be of the greatest support to you each time you open this dynamic book. At the end of each chapter you will find, the contact information and a little bit about each author. I know that they would love to hear from you, to know how their chapter supported you, and to build a connection with you through social media, etc. I encourage you to "friend" and follow those authors with whom you feel a powerful resonance and connection so that they can continue to pour into and support you on your journey in life.

Now the next step is yours. Enjoy the stories and messages that are within these pages to serve, support, and inspire you. Take the time to pause, read, and reflect. Listen to the powerful messages of hope that are waiting for you within the pages of this book. It's not an accident that you purchased this book and are opening it to read right now, today. I invite you to lean in and truly receive the messages and wisdom that will speak to your heart and soul that you will find in these transformational and dynamic pages. Enjoy this rich collection of wisdom, love, and encouragement so that you can go forth in life to Bloom Where You Are Planted and SHINE!

-----**Rebecca Hall Gruyter, Book Compiler**

Founder/Owner of Your Purpose Driven Practice and CEO of RHG Media Productions

ABOUT THE COMPILER

Rebecca Hall Gruyter is the owner of *Your Purpose Driven Practice*, creator of the *Women's Empowerment Series* events/TV show, the *Speaker Talent Search*™, and *Your Success Formula*™. Rebecca is the Network Director for VoiceAmerica's Women Channel in both radio and TV, is an indemand speaker, an expert money coach, and a frequent guest expert on success panels, tele-summits, TV, and radio shows.

As the CEO of *RHG Media Productions*™, Rebecca launched the international #1 TV channel called *Empowered ConnectionsTV*™ on the VoiceAmerica TV Network, bringing transformational TV shows and programming to the world. In March 2017, she launched her new TV Network (www.RHGTVNetwork.com) to bring even more positive and transformational programming to the world. In July 2017, she launched the Global RHG Magazine and TV Guide bringing inspirational content to the world! Rebecca is also a popular and syndicated radio talk show host and #1 International best-selling author (multiple times) who wants to help YOU impact the world powerfully!

(925) 787-1572

Rebecca@YourPurposeDrivenPractice.com
www.facebook.com/rhallgruyter (Facebook)
www.YourPurposeDrivenPractice.com (Main Website)
www.RHGTVNetwork.com (TV Network)
www.SpeakerTalentSearch.com (Free Opportunity for Speakers to get on More Stages)
www.EmpoweringWomenTransformingLives.com (Weekly Radio Show)
www.MeetWithRebecca.com (Calendar link to schedule a time to talk with Rebecca

Section 1
OVERCOMING CHALLENGES

Discover how to move through challenges, difficult situations, and discover how to SHINE no matter what comes your way. Let our authors share their wisdom, love, encouragement and practical steps to help you move through challenges and SHINE!

LIFE IS A CONSTANT CONSTRUCTION ZONE
By Dixie Bennett

It was 5:30am, a very odd and disturbing sound of bubbles, gurgling and popping, woke me from a seemingly sound sleep. I got out of bed to check it out. As I walked into my bathroom, I was horrified to see that my toilet was overflowing, and the shower was starting to fill up with blue water. Yes, I live in a condo, and yes I am on the bottom floor. I could hear that the guy upstairs was in the shower, and this particular cold winter day I was catching all the water from the apartment above. Thank goodness it was not black water! However, it was coming in fast and furious. I grabbed a couple of bowls and my recycling bin and started bailing it into my bathroom sink and running it to the kitchen. It was exhausting waiting for the guy upstairs to stop showering.

All this water, what to do? It was paralyzing and frustrating to realize I had absolutely no control over what was happening. The home that I own, and have worked so hard for, could be taken away from me in mere moments. I wanted to protect it, and I was frustrated, angry, worried, overwhelmed and tired. The man upstairs finally finished showering, and I got a break. I called the emergency number to the condo management and the process of repair and reclamation began. The restoration person called me while I was still in a panic, trying to get all my belongings up off the floor. He was kind and compassionate, and said "just do what you can". I was too busy trying to control everything, and the truth was that I really didn't have much control over anything. Oh, yeah, surrender into what is not, working for me right now!

However, as I did surrender into the process, these amazing men showed up one-by-one to do their part, each with a different style, but each calm, collected and compassionate. The plumber was the liveliest of the bunch, and flew in to save the day. He threw his coat and gloves to the floor and took charge, "Don't worry about anything, we've got this!" At this moment, there were three men cooped-up with their oversized vacuums and drain snakes in my tiny condo bathroom. The door was closed and all I could do was sit and listen to how hard these guys were working to clear this nasty blockage, and wait for the sweet sound of release. Finally, after a couple of hours of sweat and labor, the drain finally cleared and everyone was able to catch their breath, I have to admit it was a welcoming sound. They cleaned up, and to my relief, the flood was not as bad as I had feared. We were able to keep it to the bathroom, and all was right and good in the world again! Phew, I can get on with my day.

Exactly one month later, it is early in the afternoon, and I am just getting off of a call with a friend when I hear the bubbles and gurgling again! The hair stands on the back of my neck and I'm already vibrating. As I get to the bathroom, I see that water is already everywhere, the toilet is overflowing and the shower is filled again, but this time with black water!

Yuck, nothing I could do but surrender and make the emergency call.

This time it was much worse, and all I could do was stand by and observe. Thank goodness I was home, instead of being away and coming home to an even bigger disaster. The guys and their tools paraded in, (many of the same men from last time), and they were all surprised to see me again. This time the blockage was bigger and deeper, and they worked for a good twelve hours straight to fix the problem. By the time it was over, my home was destroyed. Everything had to be gutted out. Yes, I have insurance, but that doesn't diminish the feelings of anger, helplessness, grief and loss that all decided to show up in my body.

Here I am homeless, misplaced and without a permanent address to call home again! It's hard enough to go through a catastrophe once let alone a second time, and you would think it might even become easier. So, wrong!

In 2005, the same condo went through a fire. I lived in a hotel for 5 months.

This time I was fortunate to find an interim home close to my office, I chose it because it is close to the Bow River that winds through the heart of the city. From this apartment, I can see the Center Street Bridge with its lion statues standing guard, as well as a great view of the sunrise every morning. The property looked amazing based on the description and photo on the website. When I arrived, it looked exactly as the photo bonus! What I didn't know at the time was that there is also major construction going on with a new condo building right next door. I am surrounded by construction!

God sure seems to have a sense of humor. There are so many emotions that continue to come to the surface, yet I have no control over them, and must simply feel into them. My home is completely gutted and it feels violated and in a disarray. I love my sacred space and have collected items, experiences and things to make the space what it is: a sanctuary, a place to come to and be at peace.

It's my little piece of the world that is all mine.

As I look outside the window of my new apartment, I can see the ever-moving traffic, as well as the pathways along the river, which are full of people running, walking, and talking. There is so much movement! I celebrate that and observe it all. **Despite everything that is happening there are always construction zones, and everyone finds a new path around them– a slight detour. I suddenly realized that this is just how life is. We are constantly building.** Even though so much is happening with my external home; my life and business continue to flourish in amazing and brilliant ways. I have allowed myself to experience life from a very different perspective, and with that brings different experiences, relationships and connections. I have found myself reconnecting and experiencing my home city in new ways, with the opportunity to fall in love with it all over again.

I've been a great student of personal development and spiritual growth; some might even say I've entered into the path of enlightenment. Many of my clients know that I live what I teach and teach what I live. **I continue to dive deeper, uncover, release and move through.** I believe

this is a new discovery. As I continue to expand and grow in the world to fulfill a greater calling, I am to let go of attachment to material "things". My foundation has been exposed and the deep "blockages" of past baggage, conscious or unconscious, have been removed. My old roots are not serving me anymore. **I have been called to break down the container of what I knew in order to rise up with a whole new root system to take hold.**

What I know to be true is that there is much wisdom beyond our knowing that is directing us. I believe that our body is our home. When you realize, you are home, you can achieve all you need to survive right there. The shell of a physical home is just walls with a floor and a ceiling; it's what you create inside of it that is the juicy goodness: the memories. Memories live inside of us, not outside. Here I am being reminded of exactly that once again. **Each time I empty out, I expand. I call it a rebirthing process. The old version of me and all that I knew must die so that the new version can upload, expand and thrive.** Sometimes it can be overwhelming to be in the unknown; the experience is to simply be in it, surrender to it, and acknowledge it.

Here I am. I am my home.
My home is within me wherever I go, there I am.
I am home.
Breathe that in!

The foundation I thought was so secure and safe has now been dismantled and gutted. Yes, I do get to rebuild my home, but now I realize is that this experience has had more to do with me than my house. It is me being redirected. It is me being taught to detach and let go.

There is a bigger plan being created that I can't see yet. My foundation has always been me and I am learning a new way to be myself.

Throughout this healing process, I've learned another level of vulnerability by reaching out to my friends and family. I honor all the parts of me that feel scared to let go. I am learning to receive on so many levels, and most importantly, for the first time in my life, I feel fully supported. All these amazing earth angels keep showing up for me, doing their part to the best of their ability. I am loved and supported even in this turmoil. I didn't always feel that way. I had always been seeking love and support outside of myself. Through this experience I have learned that love and support is inside me, just as my home is inside me. Each time I anchor that in, I embody it and really feel it.

I could have chosen to be angry at the world and to have seen myself as the victim in this situation. However, I chose instead to see the gifts that this situation brought and continued to love myself throughout the process. I can choose fear and allow that to be my story, or I can choose to move through this with a sense of love and trust, knowing that all will be revealed as it's meant to happen. We are always in a construction zone, that is in evitable. However, you can still find your roots, allow them to anchor, and see the support that is right there unfolding in surprising and unsurprising ways, while navigating through these challenging, "construction zones."

I want to share with you some powerful information and tips to help you understand and discover some of what your body is sharing with you. I have learned over the years, both in my own health, and through my clients, that our body has so much innate wisdom, and it is giving us so many clues as to how our life, career, business and relationships are flourishing. Most of it all shows up in our *Root System*. This is our survival center, which also happens to be the first chakra. I believe that our bodies are a magnificent filing system for everything we experience in our lifetimes, be it emotional, physical and spiritual.

When we ignore the signs and symptoms, disease or illness will begin to manifest. I find most people are so numb to their body and can't feel anything from the neck down, only because it hasn't been safe to do so, and this can have so much to do with the conditioning, beliefs and behaviors we learned as children. We tend to take all the pain and hurt and stuff it down, or sweep it under the rug, instead of learning to look at it and acknowledge the pain in order to move through it.

The first chakra is known as the foundation for security and growth, and it is the one which all the other chakras can draw energy from. It is the energetic center of family, community, security, money, careers, and stability. It is physically located at the base of the spine and includes the largest area of the physical body all the way to the bottoms of our feet. Ideally we want to have a strong root chakra. It is equivalent to a tree having strong roots that are firmly planted into the earth, pulling up all the nutrients and basic elements of survival lovingly provided by mother earth. Without them, the tree would not be able to grow tall and flourish.

Sometimes people can have an over-balanced chakra that might show up as excessive energy. This might manifest in someone who overindulges in accumulating external materialistic things that are perceived to help them stay connected. It is indicative of hoarders or those who are overweight, eating way too much to feel more grounded.

When someone has an under-balanced chakra, they are not connected or rooted to the earth, and they might appear spacey or flighty. A person who spends too much time in their own head, and is overly analytical or thinks too much, is not living in the present and is not connecting with their body and earth. This shows up in physical form through poor circulation, sciatica, hip/knee pain, and numb feet. Clumsiness is also a sign of a deficient root chakra, such as tripping up or down stairs or rolling ankles. All these are signs of not being grounded to your root system or connected to your body.

What might your Root Chakra be trying to tell you?

A friend and I were walking through a local park. I discovered this amazing stump from a tree that had just been freshly cut. The bark was still alive and it gave off this amazing energy. It was an older tree because the roots were spread deep and wide; I even noticed the roots at the surface had formed in the shape of hearts within hearts (one of my gifts: I see hearts everywhere!) I knew this tree was special and I thought to myself, wow, this tree has seen and experienced so much. It has witnessed everything from people walking, families enjoying the outdoors, to the laughter of children over many generations, not to mention so many seasons and animals!

I wondered what it would be like to see through the eyes of a tree. I stepped up onto the stump, and closed my eyes. I literally felt like I became the tree, I could feel the tree wrap itself energetically around me. I felt myself become in tune with this magnificent tree. I stood for a while, and when I was ready, I opened my eyes and as I looked out over the park, just as this beautiful tree had done, it was as if I was looking through new eyes. Every color was so much deeper and brighter with a hue of deep chloroform green. I felt this overwhelming feeling of connection and of unconditional peace, and love. It was magical, I felt at home and I continue to be a tree stump meditator, and visit often.

A great way to ground and feel connected when life seems to be a constant construction zone is to find a tree stump. Take a stand, close your eyes, and just breathe. Connect with the tree and find yourself feeling more calm, balanced, and ready to take the next abundant confident and sure step forward.

About the Author

Dixie Bennett is a global change agent on a mission to empower 1 Million women leaders having had 3 neardeath experiences that lead her into the healing arts.

Dixie left her corporate career in sales and marketing to create a successful Transformational Treatment Center called Stillpoint Bodyworks, a center for wellness and empowerment. Blending energy, bodywork and coaching, she guides women to overcome pain and emotional blocks so they are freed to make their impact in the world and create joyful abundance while transforming lives.

When working with Dixie, she can see the unseen threads (your experience) woven together that create the physical experience of your life.

Overtime when these issues have not been dealt with they can cause issues in your tissues, which can lead to dis-ease or critical illness. Dixie helps you get to the CORE of your pain, find your VOICE, stand in your POWER and helps you realize that you can CREATE whatever is to happen next, opportunities are LIMITLESS and you can live a MAGICAL life. Your abundant life is waiting for you to claim it!

Dixie lives in Calgary, Alberta Canada where she has a full-time successful 'practice as well as CEO and Founder of Stillpoint Bodyworks. She is an award-winning entrepreneur, best-selling international author, speaker, mentor and teacher.

She loves red wine, giving a heartfelt hug, connecting with friends and family, traveling the world, expanding her spirituality, and personal development.

You can also find her performing 7 Bass in a local steel drum band called Calysto Steelband.

Email Address: dixie@stillpointbodyworks.ca Phone Number: 403.681.4838 Website: www.stillpointbodyworks.ca Facebook page(s):

www.facebook.com/iamdixiebennett/

www.facebook.com/StillpointBodyworks/ LinkedIn Page: www.linkedin.com/in/dixiebennett/

Twitter handle: @iamdixiebennett

CHOOSE LOVE
By Melinda Gulick

I first want to start with how incredibly honored I am to be in this Anthology. Thank you to Rebecca and my fellow authors for being on this journey with me. I look forward to the heartfelt rifts of magic that will be created by releasing this book into the world.

Can you imagine a world where all of your dreams are truly at your fingertips? You live in joy and love and get to share your gifts with everyone around you?

urrently, I serve my private healing clients helping them feel comfortable in their skin, owning their confidence and shining! We clear the gunk so they can step into empowerment and truly live to the fullest.

If you would have told me even 2 years ago that I would be living the life that I am now, I wouldn't believe you! With a lot of trust and surrender, self-excavation, hard work, and magic I am continuing to create the life that my soul is called to live.

I have outlined the steps that have helped me. It doesn't mean perfect, because nothing ever is, it means the highest version of me. I hope this serves you deeply!

Self-love, Compassion, Self- Validation-

We are responsible for being self-validators. No one else in this world is responsible for validating who we are. Eleanor Roosevelt said "no one can make you feel

inferior without your consent."

When we think a thought, we put it out into the universe so our thoughts are directly connected to our individual health and the health and happiness of this world and beyond. Our thoughts become things. Let's use our thoughts as a way to support who we are and not tear us down. With most people, women especially, we're really hard on ourselves. Take time every day to celebrate the things you've done well. Treat yourself with the gentleness and kindness that you would with a little child.

Choose Your Attitude Wisely-

No matter what the outside circumstance we can choose how we show up. A positive attitude, even in hard times, will take you a lot further than a negative one. Bad things happen in this world. Most people have been through something difficult, but we can still choose to rise above.

Don't underestimate turtles. A journey starts with just the first step. Even if the step is small you are closer to whatever it is that you desire. Small steps over time add up to GREAT things. Often we overestimate what we might get done in a few months or a year but underestimate what we can do in a couple of years.

Positive Body Image and Confidence- Currently the stats read this:

91% of women are unhappy with their bodies and resort to dieting to achieve their ideal body shape. Only 5% of women naturally possess the body type often portrayed by the media.

Body Image is closely linked to self-esteem and confidence.

This is one of my favorite subjects to talk about. I've spent years of my life struggling with my body image, through weight ups and downs, disordered eating, and compulsive exercise. I've come to a true place of peace and love with my body, but it's taken about 15 years.

This is part of what birthed my healing practice.

At a certain point, there must be a level of selfacceptance for our body shape and size. Yes, we can facilitate size to a certain extent BUT there are more important things in this world then 6 packs abs and well defined thighs. To the places of ourselves where we might feel shame, it's important to bring love. Shame in all senses of the word kills. Love heals and brings to life. Our body is a divine vessel for our soul, so let's treat them as such. See food as fuel and exercise (in healthy amounts) as medicine. Focus on how you FEEL in your body, not solely on what it looks like.

Through some of my work in the entertainment industry I've seen and experienced first-hand the pressure on looking a certain way and it's incredibly unhealthy and damaging to those in it, and to those who see the magazines, films, etc. Often "health" masquerading as you look this certain way (usually a thin woman with pale skin) and therefore you are deserving and the standard of beauty. What's called industry standard, I call bull shit and a way that the entertainment industry, the fitness industry, and our larger world controls, manipulates, and abuses the feminine form and all human bodies.

Love comes from what you can cultivate inside yourself.

When in doubt, get embodied and throw a hip circle!!

Never underestimate the power of a hip circle!!

Healing From Trauma—

Trauma in of itself is just difficult. There is no way around it. We are at a time, I believe, that the feminine wound as it has been called, is healing. The rape wound. This wounding happens to men and those who otherwise identify as well. There's no need to exclude anyone.

Trauma, especially if it happens in our young lives can affect our internal dialog. It affects the way we see ourselves and what we are willing to accept as treatment from others. It's important to remember that we are worthy, we are enough. There is nothing we have to do to be worthy.

I am convinced that untreated trauma or inadequately treated trauma is the cause of many of the issues on our planet. I've studied, explored, and implemented so many holistic and healing modalities over the years, many I now use with my clients.

Two of the most powerful are spending time outdoors and resting. Do not put pressure on trauma.

Make sure you are in your body, not hovering outside of it. Step out of the fight, flight, freeze response and into rest and relax. It's easy to reset with some long slow breaths. For those of us with body based traumas, being in the body can be scary, however it really improves over time.

It is my belief that processing through the shadow is not meant to be done alone. Perhaps that is why Maya Angelou said when one speaks she speaks for 10,000 and perhaps many many more.

It's important to remember that a healing journey is never a linear one. This path is different for everyone and that is ok.

Tapping into the Power of Community-

In my country of origin, the USA there is this notion about pulling yourself up by your boot straps. Be independent and live the American dream! Guess what, the USA is a huge and diverse country. Everyone has different dreams. People are not cookie cutters of each other.

If you want to accomplish something you do have to put the work in, but it will happen more quickly if you allow help. Great things don't happen in isolation unless you are specifically using it as intentional creation space. Tapping into the power of community that resonates with you (for me that's creative loving people with huge hearts and a desire to be of service) has expedited living the life that I truly desire. Make sure you're spending your time around people that uplift you, let go of unsupportive and overly judgemental people.

I want you to remember that there are currently 7 billion people on this planet. Whenever you feel alone, or like you can't figure something out there are a few million-people going through the same thing. Reach out, find them.

Focus on What You Desire—

What we focus on grows, truly. That's for good or for bad. You choose.

I like vision boards and mind movies. I take time every day to play out what I actually want to bring into my life. I also have a gratefulness practice. I write out the things that I am grateful for and that I feel I am doing well. Stop focusing on the things you don't want, it's a waste of time. When you do, you bring that energy into your life. That does not mean ignoring truths of this world or ignoring a difficult situations or circumstances.

Focus on how you want the journey to feel.

Take action on the ideas and visions you believe in and love and that make you happy. Dream big, but remember that dreams only come true if the vision and ACTION go hand in hand.

Highly Sensitive People and Self-Care — If you identify as a sensitive person this world can be really overwhelming. I'm certainly a highly sensitive woman.

I want to strongly encourage you to view your sensitivity as a gift. That's truly what it is. For us to function in a healthy way in this world it requires more self-care. Way more!

Take time for yourself. Learn to say no to other people.

Especially if you tend to be in a caretaker type role. Adopt the philosophy of giving from a full cup, not an empty one!

In my experience when you start to nourish yourself more, life has a certain flow. Take baths, dance, or whatever is fun and nourishing for you.

Remember your joy and pleasure are important! This is part of self-care! Joy is the highest vibration on the planet. Our greatest manifesting powers come from our joy.

I've spent years rushing around and adding too much to my schedule. I was stuck in the rut of "obligation." Rushing and enjoying rarely, if ever, go hand in hand. We live in a very fast paced world. If you're on technology all the time it's easy to feel crazy.

So, SLOW DOWN, and head up. Life is much more fun if it is taken at a pace where we can digest it. Be in the present moment and ask yourself how can I cultivate joy and pleasure now?

As highly sensitive people we are the light workers, healers, and artists. Our gifts move this planet forward. If you can harness your sensitivity and bring compassion to it then you can turn it into your power.

Trust your intuition. That still small voice. That is your guidance system, that is spirit showing you the next evolution of self. It will never lead you wrong. You've gone astray when you ignore it.

So, I want to ask you:

How do you want to serve the world? What makes you happy? What brings you alive?

What can you do in your town, city, state, country, or larger global world? What are you passionate about?

Take out a journal, put on some good music, grow your vision, bloom, and SHINE!

In the words of Oscar Wilde, "Be yourself, everyone else is already taken."

About the Author

Melinda was born and raised in Philadelphia Pennsylvania. She went to the High School for the Creative and Performing Arts for Voice and Susquehanna University for Theatre. She's studied Stress Reduction and Mindfulness at Jefferson Myrna Brind Center for Integrative Medicine, at Brendon Burchard's High Performance Academy for coaches, is a Mastery graduate from the School of Womanly Arts and has a Certification in Transformational Leadership from the School for the Transformation of Consciousness and Culture.

She's an Intuitive healer, Coach, and performing artist.

Melinda has traveled all over the world. She's a lover of people, the arts, health, and adventuring in nature and beyond. She loves working with her private clients and leading transformational events with sensual expression.

Emails- melinda@embraceyourauthenticself.com and/or mngulick@gmail.com

Phone- 267-879-6142

Websites-

www.embraceyourauthenticself.com
www.melindagulick.com Facebook- https://www.facebook.com/embraceyourauthenticself LinkedIn- https://www.linkedin.com/in/melinda-gulick-61177758/ Twitter- @mesmerlinda

Youtube-SingYourHeartOut86

Instagram- melindagulick

REMEMBER WHO YOU TRULY ARE
By Phyllis Flemings

Has something ever happened in your life that stopped you cold and caused you to rethink your life? Have you ever wondered what happened to get you off track from where you thought you were going? Have you ever just thought about settling, thinking that you can accept things as they are and be comfortable and just let your dreams and goals go? And, have you felt that you have shared your message with enough people and that they can continue making the difference that you had wanted to make?

Well, not too long ago, I went through something that I never thought I'd go through. I have always considered myself to be a positive and an upbeat person. If something happens, I look for the good and move on. The experience caused me to look at my life, re-examine it, see it and tell the truth of what was really going on. This was a painful experience because even though I am honest and truthful, I knew that I had to be very vulnerable and make changes that I needed to make.

A few years ago, I had an excellent job that I enjoyed and I was passionate about what I did. I worked for a man who gave me permission to expand and grow and really lead in a way that I felt empowered others. I had a staff of 13 people who I considered to be the best. They cared about their work and were very supportive of me, their co-workers, our leadership and the mission. I considered myself to be truly blessed. We all felt a connection with each other and felt great about the difference that we were making. After working in different parts of the organization for over 30 years, I decided that it was time for me to leave and spread the message of passion and purpose to others. I was leaving on a high note because I still felt good about the job and the people that I worked with felt good about our working relationship.

In addition to my academic training, I had been trained and had become certified as a Life and Business Coach as well as being certified as a Passion Test Facilitator. It could be life changing if a person discovered their passions and made the decision to live those passions that could lead to their purpose. I was excited for I felt that every person should know this information. I had work to do and I needed to go about doing it.

Even though, I was very happy and knew that I was making a difference, I wanted to get my message of empowerment, love, appreciation and gratitude out to more people and I felt that the best way to do that was to start my own business. In addition to using my skills and talents on my job, I was also able to work with others. Since I had a full-time position, my work with others was a gift that I enjoyed giving.

I shared my plans with people who cared for me and I trusted them to be honest. I was told that I should start this business on a part-time basis rather than resigning from my job and just jumping in with no entrepreneurial experience. I was so excited about what I wanted to do that I didn't listen. I had savings that I felt would take care of my expenses for about 18 months and I was eligible to retire. Yes, I knew that I was taking a large cut in salary but as I said, I had my savings so I went for it and knew that I was ready.

Even though I was ready and willing, my business was not moving in the way that I had hoped. I lacked skills in such areas as marketing, enrolling and really moving a business forward. I did not really know how to run my own business. I knew a lot and I wanted to share with others, however, I was one of the best kept secrets in town. I coached, I led workshops, I did public speaking and my business still stayed the same.

I attended more and more workshops, seminars, talks, and meetings. I received additional certifications. I had to understand and admit that knowing was not enough. Something was still missing. I continued to move about frantically.

By the end of the 18th month, the savings were gone and I had accumulated a lot more debt and my business was still not going forward. **Whenever I would hear of another webinar, seminar, workshop, or some other sessions that would promise the answer, I would sign up. I felt stuck and I was truly frustrated.** Notice that I was not taking time to be, I was just doing.

I believe that everything happens for a reason and I had to stop, look, and as I said earlier, tell the truth about what was going on. Yes, I asked myself those questions that I mentioned and I decided to stop long enough to get the answers. I had to remember who I was and what I taught. I had to go within and had to slow down and take time to be guided by Spirit.

I reminded myself of my trust, faith, and belief in the goodness of God. I was grateful that I had not let that go because I knew deep within that I was where I was because of the choices that I had made and that I was still here. I did review my life and remembered the many blessings that had come to me and knew that I still had the opportunity to make a difference. I still had my message and there were people who needed and wanted to hear it. I was told that these people were waiting for me.

I have a morning ritual that I do daily which includes prayer, meditation, reading inspirational material and writing in my gratitude journal. I have been doing this for years and even during those frustrating times, I continued this practice. **I decided to slow down and answers began to come to me. I was reminded of my number one passion which is to stay connected to God** *and be open*. I was also reminded of what I teach which includes knowing that we are here for a purpose and as we move forward with passion, living our purpose, the Universe supports us. We really can be, do, and have what we desire.

Having left my position, going into my own business without learning how to really run a business, going through all of my savings, being in debt, and feeling stuck caused my self-esteem to plummet. ***I was stopped cold and had to*** *rethink my life.* I knew that I had gotten off track and was not where I thought I'd be. I even though about giving up the mission and the legacy that I wanted to leave for my grandchildren. It even crossed my mind to let my dreams go for I really had shared with many through one to one discussions, workshops, coaching, and speaking my message so I could feel justified in letting those who believed in the message, go out and deliver it.

For whatever reason, I could not give up. I heard the words, "Bloom where you are planted and Shine" and the statement made so much sense to me. I looked at where I was and knew that I was meant to hear that very message. I also remembered who I was and Whose I was. I could not just stop and just let my passions die. I had to be the representative that I am here to be. I had to step up and be the person that I was created to be.

I have been teaching and training others since I was a child. I am a life time learner and love to read and grow. I genuinely care about others and look for and find the hero, the wonderful Spirit that is within them. Yes, I know the behavior is not always what we would like it to be and really, we see it and still know that the person within has what she or he needs to step up and make the difference that they are here to make. **I decided to listen and once I did that, things started to happen.**

At one time, I taught at a school where I had the opportunity to work with counselors and support them in being the type of counselor that was really available for their people. I decided to check with one of the coordinators of that school to possibly work there again. This woman had moved to another position in another area and I was given the name of a college that might be interested in my working with them. I feel that this was Divine intervention.

I went to the college and was asked to fill out an application, send in my resume, and submit my credentials. Within a short period of time, I was hired to work with these amazing people. **I am now doing what I love to do, teaching on a part time basis, sharing my message, and I feel that I am making a difference. I am also moving my business forward.** I have slowed down and am taking my learning and putting it to positive use. My people were indeed waiting for me.

I base my life on being grateful for everything that happens for I know that what may appear "bad" at the time is for my highest good so even if what is happening does not feel good at the time, I can learn from it.

I learned to appreciation people and what they do and know that we are all doing what we feel is best at the time. As I have heard many times, **"when we know better, we do better"**.

At the top of my list is to love - love God, love myself, and love others. We all know that love can overcome anything and it feels so good to love and be congruent with the Universe and who we truly want to be.

I say to all of you who read this that you are perfect as you are and **whatever mistakes or miss steps that you have made in the past, let them go for they are not who you are.** Remember that you are a child of God and you are suppose to be here. You have within you to be who you will to be; to do what you desire to do; and, to have what you want to have. **Look at those things that you don't feel

proud of as steps to your growth knowing that you are growing every day and becoming the person that you want to be.

I believe that we can all choose to live a passionate life. I support others in being clear, discovering their passions and living those passions that lead to their purpose. This is very important, for knowing your passions makes living life so much more enjoyable.

To receive a list of the "Top Five Reasons to Know Your Passions" go to www.phyllisflemings.com.

Affirmations can be very helpful. Say these daily for 90 days getting them deep into your subconscious;

I am grateful for all things. I appreciate all people.

I replace all fear with love.

I am love in human form.

I will make the difference that I am here to make.

I know that I am a co-creator with God.

I am blessed and I am a blessing

Remember who you are and whose you are and that you are needed in this world. ***Be open, slow down, listen and allow Spirit to guide you.***

About the Author

Phyllis Flemings, PhD, is a Certified Passion Test Facilitator, a Certified Business and Success Coach, and a Speaker.

Phyllis has over 30 years of experience training, teaching, and working with others to support them in seeing the awesome person that they are so that they can move forward and make the contribution that they desire to make. She believes that you already have everything that you need to live the life that you want and is patient while supporting you in seeing this for yourself.

She guides you with exercises that help you discover your passions, and find your WHY and continues to coach you in finding ways to bring your passions into reality. Phyllis has also been trained in Life and Spiritual coaching and can see that you have everything you need to bloom where you are planted and be who you truly are and desire to be.

Knowing your passions can help you feel more powerful. You will **experience** more joy and excitement and will know that you are living your life in a way that makes you happy.

You know that you have made the choice of how to live, what to do, and when and why you do the things that you do. You will stop the comparison knowing that no one can be YOU except YOU. Your passions are yours alone and even though others may seem to have similar passions, you are the only person who can really live your passions and make the contribution that only YOU can make. You have that special spark that makes you the person that you are so you can really bloom and shine exactly where you are right now.

PhoenixRising197@gmail.com
1-707-688-9097 www.phyllisflemings.com
Facebook: Phoenix Rising Again
LinkedIn: Phyllis Flemings
Twitter: @PAFRAF

LOST, LOSS AND LEARNING TO TRUST AGAIN
By Sonya Williams

There I was at the Airport in Maryland, waiting for the baggage clerk to take my luggage when she said the following words to me, "Your bag is overweight.". I nodded in ignorance and agreement because I didn't know why she was telling me this.

Then she says, "That will be $50."

At that moment, I felt like I was the main character in a movie scene who had just received bad, life-changing news. I took a sharp intake of breath as time and everything around me slowed to a halt. In that quick moment, I had to make a decision. Do I tell her that I have just been through one of the toughest and most trying 4 months of my life, and that I only have $100 in my wallet – to my name? Would she care that my 2 bags were filled to the gills with as much of my stuff I could get in them because I couldn't even afford to ship the rest of my stuff back home to California? Do I let her know about my failed job opportunity with my friend (who I had loaned thousands of dollars to) and how we had to dissolve her business and that I was going home feeling like a complete failure? No money, no job and no car. I had barely secured a place to stay for the next 3 months and that was with some stranger via Craigslist.

As I exhaled and looked into that woman's eyes, I realized how unfair it would be to her to unload this heavy, deep, dark anguish and pain. I was also afraid that I would start to cry and wouldn't be able to stop. So, I mustered up the energy to pull out the money and pay for my overweight bag.

That was me in February of 2005 at my lowest financial point in my life. I recall thinking how the heck did I get HERE?!? After all, I was a Law School Graduate, single and enjoying a pretty good life. However, I was feeling a bit lost – like something was missing from my life. I had been out to visit my best friend during the Summer and had seen how she was living the Law of Attraction. Her law office was gorgeous, she lived in a beautiful custom-built home and she had a wonderful husband and 3 amazing children. I wanted to experience what she had – or so I thought. What I later realized is that everything was not as it seemed, but in my rush to fill a void I didn't do my own due diligence. **I was too busy looking outside of myself for something instead of being clear about what it is I wanted to have for myself.** I now know **CLARITY** is key to creating and manifesting my best life.

Since I was not clear about what I truly wanted, my time in Maryland ended up being a great learning experience. That is where I begin to get clear about what I **didn't want!** As my best friend and I went through this tumultuous time we were able to talk about how we were feeling and the impact it was having on us both professionally and personally. She finally admitted that she thought I was there to save her and I admitted that I thought she was there to save me. Wow, the blind leading the blind. But hey, if you are going to go through a pretty crappy time, why not do it with your best friend you've known since 6th grade. Once you realize what you don't want, it becomes a lot easier to get clear about what it is you do want, and I no longer wanted to be in Maryland. I was ready to go home and create my best life.

As I settled into my place in California and began to look for a job something strange was happening. I couldn't get a job to save my life. In the past, this had never been an issue for me. In fact, my family often joked that if I didn't feel like I was being treated well I would leave one job and get another better one before the day was over. So here I was feeling even more lost and dealing with the loss of income, my car, my job, my stability. To make matters worse, the person I was renting from was an alcoholic who didn't like me opening the curtains during the day even though she was at work. She would also accuse me of weird random things like spilling paint on the kitchen floor. When I asked her, what would I be painting she realized how silly she sounded. I never knew who I was going to get – the sober nice roommate or the drunken, paranoid one. Fortunately, I am optimistic at heart and I began to do some soul searching. All of this crazy going on around me was not working. It was like adding salt to a very deep and ugly wound. I began to read some Esther Hicks books, joined Unity church, and began to journal again. Journaling has always been not only therapeutic for me, but also the way I connect to my Higher Self.

Over the next couple of weeks, I would begin to discover that **I had a huge money block. This money block would** prevent me from having money and abundance until I acknowledged it and cleared it up. That block, which I wore like a badge of honor, was the "I can't ask for help" block.

I was embarrassed and felt so much shame about my situation that the thought of asking for help made me break down in tears. Then there was that big pit in my stomach that left me feeling even more deflated. **Then it clicked! I was sick and tired of suffering and trying to do it all on my own. I had to trust that everything would be just fine if I actually reached out and asked for help.** So, I did...

I started by sharing with my Mom all that had happened and she reminded me that she had wanted to pay for my last year in Law School, but since she couldn't do it at the time, she began to deposit $1,000 a month into my account. Then she helped me buy a used car so I could get to my job interviews.

Finally, the energy was moving!

I was still having a problem getting a job – even a temporary one. **I remembered reading about "acting as if" I had the very thing I wanted.** I did something I would never had done and that is I reached out to a Law School friend and began to volunteer in her Law Office. It allowed me to keep up my skillset and learn something new while also being mentored by someone I admired. It also got me in the habit of getting up and going to work. It still took me a couple of months to get my full-time job, but I had the opportunity to really practice gratitude and release that energy of desperation. I was also feeling valued and needed and that helped my self-esteem too. When I did apply for my full-time job, I was feeling a lot more confident and that allowed me to bargain for a higher salary.

My next synchronicity occurred when I ran into a former boyfriend. I told him about my experience and how embarrassed I felt and he joyfully helped me out financially. He reminded me of how years earlier when we reconnected and he was having financial difficulties, I helped him without any questions asked. **I make it a policy to never judge people or their circumstances and boy that was paying off very well!**

Another key to my releasing my block was being in community! This is where Unity Church helped me to do some self-care. I began to get my Spirit fed as I showed up and was taken in by a wonderful congregation of strangers who treated me like a well-loved family member. I also got amazing support from many other friends and family members who were proud of me for taking a risk.

I could feel that my money block no longer had a hold on me. I was very CLEAR about what I wanted, I took ACTION and I asked for HELP.

I am happy to report that I currently own my home, enjoyed a wonderful corporate career that then allowed me to step into being the Money Mindset Muse I am today.

At the time, I didn't know how that experience would change my life in monumental ways. I am living my purpose of helping others discover and eliminate their money blocks. I have amazing friends that I didn't meet until this new journey began and I am surrounded by an amazing community of people who continue to uplift and inspire me. My life is GOOD!!!

I'd like to share one last thing. At the beginning of the story I shared how I had to pay for my overweight luggage. Guess where you never have to worry about the weight of your luggage – that's right first class! My international travel budget always includes first class airfare and I was so excited to be able to treat my Mother to a first class ticket many years ago too.

So here are my **Tips to Remove Your Money Blocks:**

1. Clarity - Get clear about what it is you want to experience, create or manifest. Make sure it's something that truly resonates with you – fills your heart!

2. Action - Take actions to support that desire. What actions will help you achieve your goal?

3. Connection - Finally, connect with others and ask for help. Whether it's from a trusted friend, family member or professional (coach, mentor, etc.). But make sure the people you enlist for help are able to hold your vision without judgment, criticism and with an abundance consciousness.

4. If you would like to have a chat about how I can further support you, please feel free to email me at sonya@successwithsonya.com I'd love to support your vision of your best life!

There is nothing I would change about my journey because it allowed me to bloom right where I was planted and SHINE! I wish you great success, clarity and freedom from blocks. May you remove your blocks, bloom and SHINE!

About the Author

Sonya Williams is a Money Mindset Muse, founder of Success Coaching Unlimited and creator of the Money Mindset Model. As a Money Mindset Muse, she is an expert in helping you to discover and eliminate your money blocks to create the abundance and financial prosperity you desire to live your best life. She is gifted at getting to the core issues that create financial challenges for you because she can see where the money block is showing up in your body energetically.

Her genuine passion for helping you heal your money blocks, her authenticity and great sense of humor is apparent in all that she does and that has a way of making you feel comfortable immediately. This creates a safe space that allows you to share your current financial situation openly and honestly without hesitation. That first step begins your journey of going from scarcity to abundance. As you release your negative beliefs, actions and habits, and you begin to develop a positive relationship with money, this can also impact other areas of your life in a positive way. Those who benefit most from her knowledge and experience are entrepreneurs and professionals. Sonya has a passion for making a positive difference in the lives of others in fun, practical ways.

sonya@successwithsonya.com.
Twitter - Sonya Williams @moneywithsonya

LET COME, LET BE, LET GO
By Ione Wendy Sidwell

LET COME

Where am I? What happened? Thank God, I no longer have that incessant pounding headache that I normally wake up to. Wait a minute. There's no headache? And what's that beeping noise?

Suddenly, a flood of memories and realization poured in. I'm in a hospital. I had a brain tumour. The cause of the headaches, blackouts, falls, the inability to think clearly or reason, and the weight gain. I felt a huge sense of relief. Finally, a diagnosis after a year's struggle of looking for answers to discover what was happening to me. Now, I could finally heal and get back to my normal life. Thank you, God!

I loved my normal life of being a full-time mom. Three beautiful, healthy children, 12, 10, and 8 years old. My sweet babies were verging on becoming teens, and those precious years of elementary school, soccer, hockey, gymnastics, dance, cubs, field trips, hot lunches, church, family camping, and being enfolded into a community of friendship, were the loveliest I could ever imagine.

Wait a minute. I had a brain tumor? What? Why? How did I get a brain tumor? I was healthy, fit, and happy. I don't understand. What did I do wrong? Why me? I'm a good mom, a supportive and loving wife, a solid friend, a great sis, an outstanding volunteer in the school and community. I go to church! I believe in God, and Jesus, and all the teachings. It's not right! Good, nice people like me, don't get brain tumours!

The neurosurgeon informed me that 5% of Canadians get brain tumours, and the type it was, could have been growing for 20 years. It was benign and I sighed with gratitude for that miracle. But…20 years! That meant for my whole married life, I'd had this grotesque thing growing in my head! Raising children and living what I thought was a wonderful life, a foreign mass was forming on my skull to one day take me down. It felt like my life had been hijacked by a lie of "I'm great!", when in fact, growing in my head was a heavy mass of pain and delusion.

"I will survive this", I told myself over and over. I lost my mom to cancer, when I was 17 yrs. old, and I was determined to be there for my children. Their graduations, life transitions, marriages, and families were not something I was prepared to miss, or have them miss me. This became my driving force. I was NOT going to leave my kids. Losing my mom impacted me deeply for my whole life. I had needed and missed her love and guidance every day. Her passing left a huge whole in my heart and life. "I will survive this", became my mantra.

A new and unexpected sensation hit me even harder: Anxiety. As I left the hospital, I was grateful to be alive, and still ridden with questions. "How could this happen to me? Why did it take a year to diagnosis, what if it grows back, what's this strange sensation I've never felt before, what's happening to me now?" The utter loss of control I felt over my life and body succumbing to this alien became an obsession about health, ever fearing a regrowth and wanting just to be normal again. Anxiety became a daily unwelcome visitor. At the time, I didn't know it was anxiety, and thought the symptoms and sensations were indicative of a deeper neurological problem. I lost trust in my body's health and the medical system supporting me.

For the next couple of years, I survived each day in a state of numbness, doing my best at being a good mom and wife. I coped and managed with daily routines, and was still gripped with fear at every new sensation or unexplained bodily quirk. My dear husband felt helpless and focused his energy on building a new business.

Then, I received the news I feared most of all. After a regular MRI, the neurosurgeon informed me the tumour was growing back, slowly. I instantly went into a panicked state. I fell to my knees in the underground parking, sobbing and screaming, "I can't go through this again!!!" My husband did his best, and nothing could console me. The complete loss of control was devastating.

This began my search for the truth. I was determined to heal myself. I needed to discover the meaning and message behind the tumour. I began meditation, journaling, prayer, healing courses, reading countless books on self-healing, and exploring every possible alternative healing modality.

Four years later, I agreed to have the second brain surgery. The alternative healing methods, meditation and prayer I had focused so intently on, were unsuccessful in helping the tumor disappear. I was devastated, and resigned once again to

"survive this". And, I did.

Three years after that, my children were out of high school, and were happily following their dreams. My husband was travelling almost constantly for work and I found myself alone, still fearful of another reoccurrence and having panic attacks. I felt so anxious and depressed that I wanted my life to end. I'd done a good job as full-time mom. The kids would be ok now. I could let go, and leave this life of fear. I finally agreed to start on anti-depressants and they helped me gain some semblance of normality.

The last surgery was seven years ago. As of today, the MRI's have all been clear. The anxiety occasionally pops up, and I am close to ending my dependency on the medication.

What did I learn?

Life happens. Any attempt to control my life is wasted energy. There are no clear answers. We do our best to move forward, one step at a time. I am now grateful for the tumor and anxiety that showed up in my life.

I discovered love for myself and my amazing body.

I learned forgiveness, acceptance, courage, compassion, and peace.

I learned surrender. I finally answered the question, "Why Me?" with "Why Not Me?"

I'm here, alive, well, and happily saw my children graduate from high school and university.

I feel blessed.

Let Come. We often don't understand the bigger picture our Soul and Source have for us. Whether the offering is a wonderful opportunity or a crushing life-changing moment. Let it all come.

Be willing to open your heart to the learning and experience each moment breathes for you. This life is FOR us! We are here by choice to experience it all. What we resist will persist.

LET BE

In the years, since, I've come to learn the lesson of "Let Be".

I took training and became certified as a Co-Active Life Coach. I completed a 200-hour Leadership course, and established my own successful coaching business.

Through this training, and many other supplemental courses, in particular, yoga, I learned how to become still. To honour and love whatever emotion and/or sensation appeared. Whether it was fear, guilt, shame, anger or any other negative experience, I learned how to "be with" the feeling rather than ignore it or beat myself up for feeling it. I began to trust myself again and my inner guidance.

Becoming still, connecting with my inner self, listening to my heart, and letting whatever show up, just "be there", has been life-changing. Developing self-awareness through mindfulness training, has helped with the understanding that suffering is a choice. I am willing to be with the trauma of the brain tumour, the anxiety, the uncertainty, and accept these experiences as gifts from the divine and the suffering has melts away. Now, I just feel grateful.

To 'Let Be', has allowed me to let others have their own experience of life, without me judging it, or trying to control it. I have no real understanding of anyone else's experience. I can have compassion and love, and let them go through their own experience without me labeling it from my own perspective. Then it becomes my made-up story of their experience and I make it about me. This is not helpful or true. Love is letting others be with what comes, compassionately.

Let Be. As humans, we are blessed with these highly sensitive, intelligent, multi-dimensional bodies to inhabit while here on planet earth. This gift allows us to experience all that life in this dimension brings, be it perceived as good or bad. Allowing without judgement, becoming present and loving ourselves and others, through each experience is the gift of "Let Be".

LET GO

After 25 years, my husband and I ended our marriage. Grief, loss, fear, guilt, shame, the endless stories people created, and the stories I made up of mistrust, haunted me for years. Once again, life offered me another opportunity to learn and grow. Letting go of my attachment to a marriage that wasn't serving either of us anymore turned out to be more painful than I expected, and in the end, gave us freedom to create new worlds for us both to explore.

This time I "let come", "let be" and the last piece, of Letting Go, enabled me to stand steady, focus on the light inside myself and bloom. "Let Go" was the last whisper to complete the cycle of rebirth and loving myself.

Let go of the past stories, beliefs, experiences and dreams. Let go of judgement, self-criticism, uncertainty, knowing anything as real, duality (us vs them) and of control. Instead, be present to what is here and now. Look ahead with joy and forgiveness.

Forgiveness turned out to be the healer. Forgiving myself first and then the world I had attracted for my own healing.

Forgiving the tumour, the anxiety, the lack of self-worth, the failed marriage, and even forgiving my mom for leaving us so early.

Out of the forgiveness came love. Now I can gratefully say, "I Am Love".

Steps to Blooming where you are planted:

1. **Let Come** - let life bring you whatever your soul wants you to experience for growth and learning
2. **Let Be** - trust and allow the process as it unfolds, that it is for your highest good, then, 'be with' yourself and others in the most loving and compassionate way
3. **Let Go** - forgive the stories you've made up about yourself and others, and receive the healing power of love
4. And, begin again. Everyday. This a practice, not a one-time fix.

Let Come – The Law of Attraction

Let Be – The Law of Allowing

Let Go – The Freedom of

Forgiveness SHINE! The last word in the title of this book is SHINE! *"Bloom where you are planted and Shine!"*

We each have our own journey to travel in this lifetime. And, we are also interconnected to the whole of human consciousness. When we bloom within life's challenges, we are a light that shines onto others. We contribute positive energy to collective consciousness when we Bloom and Shine, within our perceived limitations. Every time one person raises their energy; we all benefit and the world shines a little brighter. Sweet ones, Bloom and Shine! We all need each other.

"Love is letting come, letting be, and letting go." Ione

About the Author

Wendy is an entrepreneur, coach, writer, spiritual teacher and yogi. She finds passion in learning the mysteries of life, and sharing her learnings with the world!

She is a certified co-active life coach, and has over 200 hours of leadership training and development. Her coaching practice focuses on two areas: helping individuals connect with their soul or spirit for guidance in life, and understanding the importance of every relationship along their journey. Wendy is the mother of 3 beautiful adult children, and is the founder of three successful businesses. In her free time, Wendy loves connecting with her friends and family, being in nature, practicing yoga and mindfulness, and taking in what the world has to offer.

Connect with Wendy: email: wsidwell@shaw.ca
phone: 604-506-4670
website: ionelifecoach.com
Facebook: fb.me/ionelifecoach
LinkedIn: https://ca.linkedin.com/in/ione-wendysidwella91a1260
twitter: https://twitter.com/ionecoach **Instagram:** http://instagram.com/ionewendy

LET'S GET TENDER
By Marlene Elizabeth

The Quiet Vow That Transformed My Broken Financial Wings Into Feminine Power To Prosper One Brave Feather At A Time

This chapter was inspired by a letter I'd originally written as a recipe for my daughter to be rich in every way, with the intention of ensuring her financial well-being, and for positively transforming the financial destiny of our family tree. I stand for financial empowerment not only for my daughter, but for women around the world.

Needless to say, I was elated to submit the final draft for publication. For days, I poured my soul into editing and reediting the letter until it was just right. I pop the champagne, open an email to send my document, eager to celebrate and rest. It's 11:50pm, but fate has other plans. The entire letter disappears off my computer. In dire shock, I sit stunned unable to think, feel or move. I haven't lost a written log since the '90's. As a professional speaker and writer, I save everything. It makes no sense. Shock crumbles into fear and panic. I frantically scour every inch of my system searching in vain. *The full weight of reality sinks in...and I cry.*

My usual habit is to avoid emotions or buck them off with anger. This time, I allow the pain to burn through me. I weep bitterly feeling I did everything right and still things went wrong. My brain is confused. In utter despair, I feel my broken heart creep toward the doorway to quit but the 1,500 words stolen from sight still live in my bones. My blazing imagination recalls a story I read earlier that day of a mentor who suffered similar emotional quicksand -- and lived to tell the tale. In that dark hour, I'm reminded I am not alone and become aware that my brave heart is face-to-face with a choice: give up or try again. I rise still sore from the punch to my gut, six hours after some sleep, and open my laptop to begin from scratch.

I remember that self-care is essential during times like this, and stir a heaping spoonful of dark chocolate into my hot coffee. I stare at the blinking cursor on the blank screen and hear a still, small voice: "You wrote it Marlene, now **own it**". Indeed, I do. What moved me to write my letter the second time is to share the lesson I learned after writing and losing it the first time, **what matters most is what you do next.**

The beauty of ordinary feminine power is extraordinary. Even more amazing is the far-reaching design this power holds to impact the world --all from simple (not easy) choices. For women, especially, it's where our personal and financial power truly lies. Sometimes, the bravest, smartest, most valuable thing you can do is cry before you try again.

I park slowly, as song lyrics ease the restless butterflies swirling in my belly. *I have loved you for a thousand years. I'll love you for a thousand more".* Thirty minutes later, I deliver my words on stage about the day my daughter was born. I traveled to speak to 100 women entrepreneurs about "The Power to Prosper". I feel nervous presenting on this topic.

Stage fright isn't the issue. I've led many professional gatherings and workshops. This time however, I am deeply moved to share a more personal side of my success having less to do with financial statements and everything to do with becoming a parent.

Power - **so many women don't know they have it, much less know how powerful they truly are.** They lean on great strength to survive, never stepping into their amazing ability to thrive. I am in my late 30's when I hold my newborn tenderly close to my heart. I'm determined to be a stay-at-home Mom, not wanting to miss a thing. You can always create more money, but time is an infinitely precious gift, a nonrenewable resource. My spirit longs to guard her birthright to live rich in every way. **I quietly vow to raise her as a money smart girl.**

But the truth is, I feel powerless and afraid. I have no clue how to accomplish either one of these dreams, especially as a single Mom. Despite two college degrees my natural strengths, a positive outlook, a supportive community, good health, a deep faith in God and many achievements, **I suffer painfully and silently in shame over my relationship to money. Where is the prosperous woman the little girl in me dreamed, I'd be?**

Strong women tend not to reach out for help. Instead, I allow my pride and self-esteem to suffer living paycheck to paycheck, spending beyond my means, enduring sleepless nights from panic and worry over credit card debt, late fees and overdrafts, with no emergency fund, retirement plan or life insurance coverage in place. Needless to say, I avoid money conversations like bees in a garden. Years of valuable energy are spent quietly carrying my broken financial wings alone. Over time, I inadvertently create a life that leaves me broke, lost, miserable and exhausted.

Until that day, from inside my own body, a miracle arrives, my daughter! Her beautiful life fuels my courage and creativity to break through fears and doubts, renewing my faith to succeed. I realize that, much like my own parents,

I didn't learn money management skills in school or at home.

The money habits I develop arise solely from pure observation. Those habits become part of me without much thought, some positive, but mostly self-defeating.

I dive into the waters of financial literacy, learning all I can about building wealth, while privately questioning if I'm smart enough to understand the foreign world of business and numbers. After all, (I believe) "*I'm not good at math*". Thanks to an excellent book, I discover a valuable secret; personal finance is not rocket science, it's about making positive, informed choices. Information is a great start, yet I remain in financial woe which leads me to a deeper dive. I am surprised to discover that financial education isn't the only ingredient for healing my relationship to money. **I realize that abuses of power I witnessed in childhood invisibly ultimately hinder me from standing in my own power in adulthood.**

Gratefully during prayer one day it registers in me that, *money is like water; ordinary, extraordinary and essential to life on earth.* This reframe of power gradually releases my fears of financial success. It restores freedom for me to explore my earning potential and grow abundantly. **Like all journeys filled with twists and turns, learning about wealth turned my understanding of money** inside out. Never did

I expect the key to financial happiness sat beneath my nose waiting for me to find it. Because of motherhood, I did. **With deep gratitude, my wholehearted prayer is that you, dear reader, discover that the golden egg of financial ease already lies within you.**

Love is the key behind my success and my will to rise. Behind every cash flow statement, every break-even point, every early morning and late night, every win, learning experience and sacrifice, the power that launched my business and keeps it running, is my love for my daughter. I did not consciously realize I was stepping into my power to lead change -- a *seachange*- - in the course of her life and mine. I only knew my determined desire to give my daughter an even stronger foundation than I had growing up. I want her to know that she's never, ever alone.

So now I ask you to close your eyes. Think of your favorite scent. Inhale it deeply. Let it fill you, then exhale peacefully and open your eyes. Cup your hands together as if thirsty for a drink, and then bathe this blessing over you: *money isn't about paper, it's about people and people are designed to soar in every way.* Design your life to spiritually and financially rhyme.

I've learned that we as women are naturally equipped with the most beautiful tools to prosper: *visibility* {when we allow ourselves to be seen}, *vulnerability* {when we step beyond our comfort zone to connect with others} and *value* {when we know our unique strengths and how to use them in service for others}. I call this combination of tools "money wings", which is our feminine power to prosper. It's time to bloom and shine! Here are 8 of my favorite mindset practices to help you start to grow money wings, one "brave feather" at a time.

1. **We create what we <u>BELIEVE</u>.** One of the most successful women I heard speak gave a lesson full of key points. At the end of her talk, each point led to her core message: "If you believe, you will succeed." She led a billion-dollar company. (Rarely did I blink as she spoke.)

2. **90% of success is <u>IN</u> how you show up.** Be ever mindful of your thoughts, words, actions and habits for they lead to your character and destiny. Create an environment around you that supports your success including your physical space, mindset, routines, and the people you allow (and don't allow) into your space. Surround yourself with those who believe in you and energize you to blossom. Sit in the driver's seat - take full responsibility for your life and wellbeing.

3. **Live in <u>YOUR</u> full potential to shine.** Avoid "comparison-its". The illusion I followed trying to be like everyone else only lead me in circles! Move forward instead, pouring your energy and focus into being someone you love. Know your purpose, your clear desired outcome and daily inspired actions to achieve it. Be the honest channel you can only be, and then allow the Universe to take care of the rest. (You'll be astounded at the miracles you'll experience!)

4. **Be <u>BRAVE</u>.** Self-limiting beliefs are like sticky goblins --they become so much a part of you, you don't even realize they're there. When you're stuck in frustration, unable to move past your fears and tempted to settle - don't. Instead, ask yourself, "what if..." One of the bravest questions I asked is "what if

I can be spiritual *and* wealthy?" The truth set me free. "A comfort zone is a beautiful thing, but nothing ever grows there". Friend courage.

5. **The <u>HEART</u> of financial success lies in relationships.** *I cannot emphasize this enough:* know your value and self-worth. Honor your feminine leader qualities to create, nurture and transform!

6. Women are especially gifted in building relationships. You are empowered to generate amazing income and impact in the world. Know that you already have *everything* to begin and you'll experience financial freedom quicker than you can imagine.

7. **You <u>AND</u> I cannot accomplish great things alone.** We need others to achieve the greatness we were born to share. Brain science reveals the valuable ways we need a support team to shine in our full potential as individuals and as a society. The beauty of "left brain", "right brain", male and female teams working together is essential for creating unlimited possibilities to thrive.

8. **Honor your <u>BLAZING</u> zone of genius.** Everybody has a gift - trust yours. I've always seen the world through eyes of faith and innovation, but greatly undervalued these strengths based on the opinions of others. As a result, my world became very small and financially unstable. When I learned to be vulnerable in safe places to connect with others, opportunities "magically" appeared. Live in your unique design and you'll soon ignite a flourishing, joyful life.

9. **Value the world of pure <u>IMAGINATION</u>.**

10. Guard your freedom to view life not only as it is, but as it could be. When you struggle trying to figure out "the how" of a situation, remember Einstein who said, "We cannot solve problems with the same thinking we used when we created them". Focus on the outcome you wish to achieve, and "the how" will present itself to you

(Believe In Your Brave Heart And Blazing Imagination.) My dear amazing reader, thrive! Not for financial gain alone, but from your call to be authentically YOU. You will never find your personal power in money. You find it in the personal choices you make. What matters most, is what you do next!

About the Author

Marlene Elizabeth inspires heart-centered women and visionary leaders to thrive by design. Through her private 1x1 coaching program Courage To Soar™, she helps clients "break the shell" with a fresh perspective to answer their call to greatness in business and life, one brave feather at a time. Despite her introverted nature, Marlene expands like an extrovert beyond her comfort zone in life, leadership and entrepreneurship. At the tender age of 19, she traveled 3,000 miles away from home to work on Capitol Hill for former U.S. Congressman Leon Panetta {at a time when the current global technology that keeps us so well connected, did not exist}.

The same is true when she left the security of her 9-5pm job {and never looked back} to volunteer for one year at her local church, she said, yes to co-hosting a National TV show on TBN that aired in 100 million homes around the world (before video broadcasts everywhere on YouTube + Facebook) and drove a 36-passenger sight-seeing trolley giving tours through the narrow streets of Boston (as a California transplant), and gave birth to her beautiful daughter at the age of 39.

Marlene understands the riches that lie beyond our comfort zone, the inherent fears and challenges we face traveling into the unknown, and the magic that happens when we dare believe in our brave heart and blazing imagination to bloom, and shine. She earned her Master's degree in Religious Education from Boston College, her B.A. in International Relations from U.C. Davis and is a Certified Brain Personality Specialist. Marlene is a special featured contributor for the book *"Dear Amazing Daughter"* due for release in 2017. She's the author of *Women of the Millennium* video series, in English and Spanish, used in over 150 churches and media centers worldwide, including Africa, Ireland, Canada and the U.S.

marlene@marleneelizabeth.com 909.247.1127
www.marleneelizabeth.com
www.facebook.com/rekindlewithmarlene

Section 2
STAND IN YOUR TRUTH

Discover your truth, and how to stand powerfully in it and SHINE! Gain tips, tools, and insights to help equip and empower you to stand in your powerful truth.

CHOOSE TO BLOOM
By Teresa Hawley Howard

Life has lots of valleys and peaks. Highs and lows. Your heart soars and your heart grieves. It can truly be a roller coaster ride. It can be a whirlwind. We must learn to love each place we find ourselves occupying. Each season as we travel through it. We can find ourselves in situations we never imagined. In jobs, relationships or places where we are not content. Where we do not feel like shining. Where we don't feel like blooming or growing. But we must! We must continue on our journey. And we must always be giving our best. Giving our all.

I know you are saying, "yeah, right!" I can't even function. I don't see the end in sight! I am so overwhelmed and suffocating! I know that feeling! I have been there! I was stuck! I was hurt! I was sure it was the end. The end of my dream! The end of vision! And definitely the end of my business! But it was not! It was only a valley, a detour, a roundabout way to my destiny! Just another adventure and path. But I had to embrace it! I had to choose to let go how

I thought it was supposed to look like! I had to accept it and choose to blossom! Choose to use my lessons to change lives. To take the hardships and turn them into victories!

You can choose this too. I know you can do it! I have faith in your abilities! In your heart! In your endurance! You can either complain, be depressed and bitter. You can choose to let your pain and past to define or let it propel you! I have learned to choose to thrive! I had to choose to let go of the past and the pain and to move forward. I know I have a purpose. I want you to understand how important is to let go! To bloom in each season! Our lives are always going to be hectic and crazy. There will be times when we think we cannot go one more day! I promise you that you can! I know you can! I believe you can!

Let me tell you about my journey. I had a very unconventional childhood. I grew up very quickly! My father was a heroin addict and never there for me. I cannot even remember living with him as a child. My mother assures me that we did. But there are no memories with him. He chose to walk away. That does a number on a little girl. But instead of rebelling, I went the other way. Straight A's in school. Looking for approval there. Because I did not get it at home.

My mom chose the wrong men. Which meant our lives were usually chaos! And unstable. I stayed with my grandparents most of the time. It was my sanctuary. My hiding place. My anchor. They loved me. Poured into me! Praised me! They were the ones who told me I could do anything! The first ones to praise me! The first to help me see my potential. I believe we all have those angels in our lives. I just happened to be related to some of mine. But they were not my only ones. I had teachers who saw my potential. And told me!

Who helped to build me up and show me another side of life? I believe in all seasons of life; we have people placed to help us.

Can you think of someone who was there for you? Who encouraged you? Who inspired you? Who knew your potential, even before you did? Someone who help you blossom even in rocky soil? Well I know if you think about you have at least one! Be sure and thank them. Acknowledge all they have done for you!

I was a little girl from the wrong side of the tracks. No money, no family name, not supposed to succeed. Destined to fail and be a statistic! But that did not happen. My destiny and success was delayed but not denied! I endured a lot! A rough childhood. An abusive marriage. And cancer twice! But I overcame! And along the way I choose to bloom. To do my best. To be a friend. To be an encourager! To speak love and life into others! As we walk through our life, we will be given chances to sow seeds. To sow into other lives. Take those chances! Do it! You will never regret seeds sown. And eventually those seeds will take root. They will blossom! They will help another. And the best thing we can do with our life is inspire another.

Just start from where you are. No matter where that happens to be! Choose to bloom. Choose to shine. Small steps in the right direction count! Every single step toward your goal, is huge! Maybe today it's just getting out of bed. Tomorrow maybe getting dressed and going out! Each day make progress. I have been in the pit! I know failure. I know defeat. I know sorrow. But I also know success. I know victory! And I know JOY! And so, do you. Life may deal us blows, curves and detours. But it is how we react to them that matters. How we choose to handle it. What we do when we are pushed. How we handle the tough situations.

Our lives are forever evolving and changing. So, we must learn to embrace the seasons. To love our lives. Each season is a chance to make a difference. A chance to change lives. A chance to bloom! A Chance to be the light! A Chance to be a blessing. A Chance to learn, grow and prosper. Each of us can do something spectacular! Each one has a purpose! So, find yours! And pursue it with a passion! Life gives us times to be the champion. So, take it! You know you were meant to shine! You were meant to be great! If no one has told you! I will, you are amazing!

Life is always an ebb and flow. It will have sunshine. It will have rain. But both are needed to bloom. You must plant, nurture, water and be prepared to bloom. Just like in a garden, life is a cycle. It is always moving. We must learn to flow with it. To remain still is to become stagnate and stifle! So, keep moving, keep growing, keep learning and embrace your season. Learn to turn your tribulations, your trials and your problems into lessons. Maybe you will learn from them or you will share them and millions will learn from them! Your choice! Your decision!

I hope my story and my life inspire another. I hope it gives light into the darkness. That you read it and you see yourself in my story. That you say I can do it. I can choose to bloom. I can choose to make a difference. I can choose to be the change. The ripple in the pond! To be one who spoke up and changed the world! You can! I believe in you and in me! So, let's change the world together! Join me and let's bloom together!

My tips to help you bloom and SHINE:

- Choose to Bloom.
- To make a conscious choice each day to make it happen.
- To make your life what you want it!
- You must decide to become the change you want to see in our world.
- The best way to do this is one choice at a time.
- The choice is yours to make!
- No matter how small the step!
- It is a step in the right direction.
- It's a step toward your dream and your future.

About the Author

Teresa Hawley-Howard is a domestic violence survivor and an advocate. Her mission in life is to help other women find their voice and share their stories! She also wants to help them walk through their pain, limitations, and their own doubt to live the life they deserve. She knows their words, stories, scars, and their pain can inspire, heal and give hope to another woman. She is an empowerment/writing coach, speaker, #1 international best-selling author, radio host, and CASA volunteer. She is also Co-Founder of Tribute Magazine, spotlighting women. Founder of Women on A Mission, inspiring and uplifting women to live the life they desire. Radio Host of WOM Radio show, and host of Modern Day Woman Podcast! Teresa's goal is to help 10k women share their stories! Reach out and let Teresa help you share your story!

She is also the founder of Women on a Mission Enterprises. WOM Enterprises offers complete publishing packages for authors! The company offers several ways to become an author! You can write in one of many anthologies or you can write your own book! Either way you will become a published author! Share your story, promote your business and create your legacy! WOM Enterprises will help you make your dream become a reality. So, stop procrastinating and become an author today with Women on a Mission Enterprises.

teresa@takeactionwithteresa.com
www.teresahawleyhoward.com
903-910-9635

SECRETS WORTH TELLING
By Brandy T. Jones

It came to me in a dream. The story was a vision of me being between the lines in the center of a long road. I didn't know which side I should go to, which side would accept me, on which side did I belong?

This experience of feeling like I was in the middle of the road began when I was four years old. I knew I was different than the other girls who played "House" and "Doctor" with the boys at preschool. Even at this young age, I preferred the company of girls. In our games, I envisioned what it would be like to be a grown up living my life with another woman. I already appreciated being in the presence of feminine beauty. I felt a sense of compassion and gentleness sharing with females that I never felt with males. It seemed right to me to blossom with other flowers, creating a spectacular field.

Having intimate feelings about girls' bodies was my deepest secret until my early 30's. My first physical experience with a woman was one of my choosing. We had been friends for years. I wasn't even sure if she was a lesbian, because we had never talked about it, and I didn't even have that language for it, when I asked her if she liked women. She said yes. In time, I invited her to dinner, and after our first encounter, I felt a kind of completion I had never known before. The visions from my dreams had come true, and I felt that blossoming field coming alive within me.

Blossoming though, can have a price we each must be willing to pay. I really don't know how my family will interpret this chapter. My decision to publicly reveal my secret began with a discussion with my daughter. She has been an integral part of my learning to be a complete woman: wife, mother, grandmother, friend and partner. I wanted to be sure to respect and honor both her and myself in this mission to tell my story to readers who have likewise felt in the middle of life's long road. While my family "accepts" my lifestyle, I have rarely introduced my partners to them. They never met my first female partner though our relationship lasted five years.

My first female relationship began after I had already been divorced from my husband for over ten years. I had still been dating men, but something was missing. I felt out of place. It seemed the common thread was my relationships with men, I decided I should try an adult relationship with a woman. Like any relationship, gay or straight, people change, the relationship shifts, and there is an option to move on.

Though I chose to leave her, over the years we remained friends. That first relationship opened my eyes and heart to the possibility of finding a love so complete that it could last. Stepping out of the box of my old beliefs created a change, and with it the beginning of a different life. Years later, **I**

realized my choice wasn't even about who my partner was, but more of how I related to myself.

Fear was a big part of my staying straight for as long as I did. Without anyone to look to as a lesbian role model, I looked for other representations of successful relationships. What I saw was that they were built on a foundation of telling the truth. This belief led me to consider "coming out" as the ultimate test of personal integrity. **I took on the challenge – one person at a time.**

There are generally people with whom we feel safer to share our truth, or in this case to "come out." Which lead me to question, what does it really mean to be "out"? Because that kind of honesty is a two-way street. When I come out to someone, it brings them out with me. Whether gay or straight, people create intimacy by sharing truthfully, by coming out to each other with their deepest secrets. This closeness builds relationship, and when it is absent, creates distance instead.

When I was married, I did the "right thing" by marrying a man and having a family. I knew there was something "more" that I wanted but I didn't know exactly "what" at the time. The "more" turned out to be feeling complete, connected, safe and at home within myself and within my relationship in a way I'd never known before. The "what" was secretly admiring, loving and wanting my primary relationship to be with a woman.

It seems ironic now, that I lived much of my life as a straight person in a gay world. I accepted being a woman, secretly knew I wanted to love a woman, and still had to learn I didn't have to prove I was any other way. When I made the decision to live as a lesbian, in both worlds the longing stopped and the questions were answered. Except for one: how do I live "out there" the way I have been behind closed doors?

My house today is one of open doors. It is a representation of the diversity I've lived. As a black woman in a white world, it never dawned on me that I shouldn't be there. The color of my skin only became an issue when someone brought it to my attention by behaving toward me as if I were different. Living in other countries enabled me to take advantage of a variety of cultures. I engaged with communities which supported me in doing more than the locals of their own hometowns. This vast array of experience has opened my thinking, my relationships and the very fabric of my living space.

There are both Asian and African influences in my home, which represent to me the nature of ancestral villages: respect for family, for elders, for oneself, and for the generations to come. My environment embraces a deep sense of continuity and lineage, which places my finite life within the infinite wholeness of the world.

For all the complexity of relationships, life itself is at its roots elemental. **We are given the gifts of our life and those we share it with. Even my plants remind me that growth requires cultivation and connection.** Whenever they aren't doing well, I am prompted me to get down to the earth, create balance with water and the sun's fire, in the presence of fresh air. Much like a plant, as we grow we change, we and our relationships expand and flower, and move through cycles of life, death, and rebirth.

It is to the recognition of these cycles that I've learned to live without regret. I know that living the life I have chosen (being married and having my daughter, coming out as a lesbian, becoming an entrepreneur and more) is what allowed me to become the person I am today. For this blossoming, I am thankful for all the phases of my life. Free of regret, I allowed myself the freedom and opportunity to create a different life, unbound by past limitations. I allowed myself to truly shine in my own life.

If you were to look at me, you might label me as a black woman, but you might not immediately see me as a lesbian. In the middle of the road, I don't appeal to the typical stereotypes. From either side of the street, both straight and gay people have told me I don't "look like a lesbian." Even when I identify with a group, they don't accept me as one of their own based on how I look on the outside. There is no consideration of how I feel on the inside. No accounting for my personal truth.

Going deeper within, I sink into my truth. I don't know what could possibly be deeper than this long-held secret revealed, an identity with and without labels, and a commitment to a life of no regret. **Without feeling like I should blend-in, I can accept myself regardless of appearance or preference. I know that being different brings compassion for myself and permission for others, to find our own tribes, which may not fit any one particular mold.**

Outwardly I fit into various individual groups, but inwardly my puzzle picture is more diverse than any one group can hold. Coming out of the closet, my pieces started to come together. I started to figure out who I am, how I belong, how I live my life for me. When my picture came together, it revealed how **living from my center allows me to make** the most of interacting with my various communities and the world at large.

I've come a long way since that four-year-old-girl in the middle of a metaphorical road. Today, I know where I stand, and it's neither here nor there. I am in the middle of the road by choice, and am comfortable not being identified as coming or going, in or out, straight or gay, because I am complete inside. Decisions come easier, because I make them for my best interests. I know that my actions have consequences, and have turned the table on my choices, such that I now say, I view my consequences first to direct my actions toward the consequence of my choosing.

If I could go back in time, I would whisper to that little girl in the road, "it's safe to be who you are, it's safe to trust in beauty, it's safe to connect to the softness of women that you love." I would whisper to my 19-year-old-bride-self, "This marriage will bring your daughter, your greatest gift." I would whisper to my thirty-something seeker, "Follow your heart and set your secret free."

This is the same advice I give to you now. If you're not sure of what your heart wants or what your secret desire is, be quiet and listen to the sound of your inner voice. Shut your ears to the outside world, and open to the love which is yours for the taking inside your own being. If only to yourself for now, tell the truth, and in so doing, deepen your inner intimacy, which will in time, expand into your outer relationships. Revealing to ourselves our own secret longings, and owning the dreams and visions of our youth as the adults we have become, brings us into a place of wholeness.

One of the ways I can support you on your journey is through my international radio show, "Journey to Balancing Your Life," I invite guests from all walks of life to share their stories, perhaps some secrets truths, which have the potential to become pearls of wisdom for all of us. I would love to have you listen in, be inspired, and empowered on your beautiful life journey as you discover how to bloom and shine! You can find the show on www.VoiceAmerica.com, every Thursday, 11 am12 noon PST (plus archives…so you can listen on demand…for free to any show that would be of support to you or your friends). In a world that tends to keep each other at arm's distance, it is my goal to creative a supportive community where we can show up as ourselves and know that we are not alone. My love and support to you on your journey! Please find some tips to support you listed below.

Brandy's Tips to Bloom & Shine:

- It is safe to be who you are
- Trust in beauty of how you are made
- Follow your heart
- Listen to your inner voice and honor yourself
- Set your secret free within yourself, own it, and stand in it
- Be part of a supportive community
- Allow yourself to shine in who you are this is a gift to yourself and the world!

About the Author

Brandy Jones has always been an entrepreneur and educator. At the age of seven she started her first business, which planted the seeds of her first savings account, and thus began a legacy of financial empowerment. In a military family, she relocated often and became adept at building new relationships with ease. It is this instant rapport that her diverse clientele share with her today.

Ms. Jones accepts where her clients are without judgment. Having faced her own struggles with debt head-on, Ms. Jones learned to negotiate with creditors, manage a budget and rebuild her savings. She has walked in the shoes of being heavily in debt and for her filing bankruptcy was not an option. She wanted more than a quick fix.

Brandy Jones, CEO of End the Red, has a mission to empower others to live a financially sound life, and her vision is to educate the youth of today to be fiscally strong adults of tomorrow. Ms. Jones will assist those who are having difficulty with their credit and give them new choices through training and education. She has a unique way to get people to talk about finances, how they feel and look at the big picture and from there make sound decisions.

End the Red is the business where the client will feel empowered to continue to handle their finances in a more responsible matter. Thus, End the Red's *purpose is to provide clients with a very personal and educational path on how to budget, how to maintain control with credit, and to develop a savings plan.*

Journey to Balancing Your Life, Brandy's international radio show, is successful in over a dozen countries. Her show brings practical tips for living in a balanced way together with inspirational guests from all walks of life. Many episodes pull from Brandy's co-authored books, "Discover Your Destiny, Live Your Dreams, Love Your Life," "Come Out of Hiding and Shine," "Women Warriors Who Make it Rock," and her upcoming addition, "Bloom Where You're Planted and Shine," Her repertoire of events includes her public appearances, which bring her stories and wisdom to life. brandy@endthered.com

510.520.1715 www.EndtheRed.com
www.facebook.com/5DollarsBecauseUmatter
https://www.linkedin.com/in/brandytjones

AN OLYMPIAN'S MINDSET
Winning Defined Differently
By Coach Sherry Winn

In 1988, I was 27 years old, living the dichotomy of thoughts most young women have, between the zone of confident and poised, and insecure and angst-ridden. Despite my wavering emotions, I was about to play in my second Olympic Games in Seoul, Korea.

Most athletes dream about being an Olympian but only a handful of the best make the cut. Despite being a two-time All-American and a valedictorian at the University of Charleston, I refused to describe myself as good. I was a minimizer. I excelled at taking an event and minimizing it to the smallest extent possible.

My rationalization went something like this:

- ✓ The only reason I made the Olympic team was because I played a sport, team handball, that few Americans played.

- ✓ I was valedictorian at a small, liberal arts university. There were less than two thousand students, so it wasn't a big deal.
- ✓ I was All-American and two-time conference MVP in college, but I was older than most my teammates so I had an advantage.

How many times have you diminished your accomplishments and why did you reduce them?

Were you afraid that you were going to be labeled "Cocky or Arrogant?" Or did you have a voice inside you whispering that you were not good enough, and the only way to align with that feeling of not being good enough was to minimize your accomplishments? Even though I had a room full of trophies, ribbons, and awards, I never saw myself as a great athlete. Why did I do this? The same reason most people tell stories about themselves—I possessed limiting beliefs about my past that I held as truth. One of my limiting beliefs was that nobody liked me. I developed that belief as a young child when my mother sang the Worm Song to me. Maybe you've heard the lyrics to the song:

"Nobody likes me. Everybody hates me. I'm going to eat some worms. First you get the bucket, then you get the shovel. Ooh, how they wiggle and squirm."

Imagine how singing that song over and over in your head would make you believe that your teammates and coaches hated you. If you sang that song from the time you were two until the age of 30, you might realize that the song was holding you to a story that kept you belittled and dismissed by others. The Worm Song created the belief that people hated me, perpetuating me to take actions which caused people to find me undesirable.

My belief that nobody liked me came to full manifestation during the 1988 Olympic Games. When we arrived at the Olympic Village, my head coach, and I had our differences. He was 50 years of age, a Hungarian, and a hardcore believer in pushing his team to the limits.

Our national team trained year around, twice a day, five days a week and once on Saturday mornings. Coach believed that we had to train as hard as we could every single day so that we would have a chance at winning a medal.

I was a type A personality, a driver, and a go-getter, but even I recognized the diminishing returns of pushing players too hard. Several of my teammates were sidelined due to ongoing, chronic injuries, and many of us suffered from the classic symptoms of overtraining including headaches, inability to sleep, weight loss, and fatigue.

One practice after coach ran us for the entire two hours, I cautiously approached him. "Coach, can I talk to you?"

"Yes. Please. You talk."

"Coach, we are exhausted and need a break. We can't think. Heck, we can barely move."

Coach's face reddened as he yelled, "You don't know training. We must to train hard, harder, hardest. You no coach. Don't know nothing. Now go."

The two of us never recovered from that conversation until I signed a contract with the United States Team Handball Federation two months before the Olympics to be his assistant coach after the Games. Then, Coach looked at me differently.

Too differently.

Coach no longer glared at me but winked at me, furtively touched me, and made faces that felt like a pick-up line in a bar.

I ignored his come-ons.

Maybe you've never experienced your boss, supervisor or coach flirting with you, but if you have, you probably had the same questions I had. How do you get him to stop his sexual advances and still get to play, or in your case, keep your job? Maybe you think you are a strong person. I did. But no matter how strong you think you are, when you are placed in a comprising position, your lines of strength become blurry. By the time, we arrived at Seoul two weeks prior to the games, I was leery of Coach. His sexual advances were covert enough that none of my teammates noticed them, but I believed he was crossing the delicate line between coach and player. I no longer had to guess whether he was crossing the line when I found myself alone on an elevator with him.

When I stepped into the elevator, I was relieved to see our team leader talking with Coach. With her in the elevator I knew I was safe, but when the elevator dinged for the second floor and our team leader stepped off, my mind froze.

You've been there, haven't you—when you know you should act but your mind won't move? Your mind is in a stalemate, in that lingering space between a question and a decision. By the time my mind reached the conclusion that getting off the elevator was my best option, Coach had made his move, grabbing my arm, preventing me from escape. When he spun me around, he didn't say a word, but instead covered my mouth with his. I closed my eyes and prayed.

What I didn't do and what the lawyers later told me I should have done is tell him to stop. Make no mistake that I didn't return his kiss, nor take any actions to invite more of him, but

I didn't yell, scream, bite, kick or say, "NO!"

How could I?

He was the one who determined whether I played in the Olympic Games or not.

Saved by the ding of the elevator and the opening of doors, coach stepped out as if nothing happened. Maybe he felt nothing happened, but to me, my life was irrevocably changed at that instant.

I didn't exactly bloom at that instant, nor for several years later, but that instant was the beginning of a journey to align my inner being with worthiness.

You might be on your journey right now, the journey to bloom where you shine. You might not recognize the light that is shining on you, most people don't, but you are on a journey to find the best within yourself. Every event that occurs to you is happening __FOR__ you even if you cannot understand the opportunity yet.

Coach didn't stop with the elevator kiss. He found ways to covertly corner me, kiss me, and caress me during the next week. I quietly accepted his come-ons…until the day he didn't play me in a scrimmage game, because he pushed his flirting too far and I snapped back at him.

Coach retaliated at my words by not playing me in the scrimmage game against the Russians. Since Coach wasn't playing me, I had nothing to lose.

After deliberating all night, I took my story to the team. And, my teammates betrayed me. Totally and completely. Their concern was that I was going to ruin their opportunity to win a medal. One of my teammates said, "You can't tell anybody. Coach will go crazy." Another one said, "This is the Olympic Games. Can't you just ignore him?"

Have you ever been so traumatized, held under fear and intimidation that you looked the other way? Have you ever wanted something so badly that you pretended not to know, so you could justify your desires?

My teammates and I wanted to play in the Olympics so badly that we accepted emotional and physical mistreatment for the honor to compete.

Without the backing of my teammates, I was a lost soul. I drank whiskey at night as a sleeping aid, cried when nobody was looking, and played brave when they were.

We didn't win a medal and my career ended in a sham. The last game I played as a national team member, Coach yanked me from the game, screamed that I had ruined the Olympics for everybody, and banished me to the end of the bench. When I refused to go to the end of the bench and instead sat down with my teammates, Coach threw a temper tantrum, left the bench, and sat in the stands, refusing to coach us.

At half time, the federation president came to the locker room, accused me of ruining the Olympics for the team and the nation, put Coach back in charge of the team, and left me imprisoned in the locker room with two federation officials standing guard at the door.

The shame and embarrassment I felt, the abandonment by teammates, and the betrayal from Coach and the federation spiraled me into a deep, dark depression. Suicidal thoughts framed by self-hatred and loss of respect for mankind were daily companions.

After the Olympics Games, the federation fired me from my position as assistant national team coach for insubordination during the 1988 Games. The federation officials claimed that I disobeyed Coach during the last game and caused national embarrassment.

In my mind, all that mattered to me, was shattered.

When you are in that desperate place, believing that nothing possible could shine in your life again, you have two options: love yourself more deeply or continue to believe in your unworthiness. Which one would you choose?

I choose to honor myself presenting the claim to the Office of Civil Rights that I was fired, because I came forward with allegations of sexual harassment against Coach. The federation fired back with allegations that I was a disciplinary nightmare, belligerent and disrespectful, a player who told lies, created team dissention and who had a history of affronting coaches.

With my OCR representative, I met with the U.S. Team

Handball lawyers to discuss the accusations. The federation lawyers fired accusations at me, retold every incident that happened during my seven years with the national team and in every story brought out the word, "homosexual." They even claimed that I could not have been harassed because I was a lesbian. Within fifteen minutes, the OCR representative terminated the meeting.

Maybe these words would not be so damaging today, but in 1988, being branded as a lesbian would have prevented me from coaching a high school or college team. In 1988, people believed a lesbian would pass her "disease" onto their daughters, and no parent wanted that to happen to their child. I dropped the case against the US Team Handball Federation and went into exile.

I spent weeks crying, lost in despair, not talking to anybody, barely moving, plotting for ways to disappear, hoping that somehow the feeling of betrayal would dissipate, and that my heart would heal again. In the center of all the pain, I hated myself. I wanted to punish myself for not being good enough, for not having the right words or the right actions. I knew at the center of my pain was me, and that damned Worm Song that my mother sang to me all those years ago, was right.

Nobody loved me. Everybody hated me.

How often have you felt this way—that life wasn't fair, that people were out to hurt you, that you wanted to disappear, that you didn't know if your heart could take another hit? **And then, in your agony, you made the whole situation your fault. You thought if you used different words or reacted a better way that you could have avoided the hurt. And because you failed to do those things, you deserved to be tortured.**

What changed for me? How did this event serve me and help me bloom so I could shine? How can my story serve you? I shared my journey with you, because you've probably experienced a pain so deep that you believed you would never get through it. You can.

Sometimes the loss of everything that is important to you is the path to freedom. Sometimes the only way you learn is to experience a pain so deeply that the pain causes you to wake up to a new awareness. Pain is your messenger. Pain tells you to look for other options, to search deeper, to open your heart in a way that it has never been opened.

What miracle occurred to take me from misery to happiness, from despair to exultation and from sorrow to bliss? I chose to reinvent me just like you can reinvent you. I read self-help books, talked with mentors, wrote in journals, joined support groups, voiced self-affirmations, expressed gratitude, and uttered prayers of forgiveness.

The process to find and support a new you so that you can shine won't happen in a day or a week or a month. The process might appear slow, because you can only take the steps you are prepared to take.

You can't jump from anger to joy in a day, nor from grief to forgiveness. What you can do is commit to the process and trust that the steps you take are the right ones for you now. I became a national championship coach, award-winning speaker, and Amazon best-seller because during my transformational process, I learned forgiveness, humility, empathy and self-love. I'm able to give more to other people because I learned the value of giving to myself.

You can move through and beyond whatever heartache you are currently experiencing. I am here to support you so you can bloom to shine. You were born to be a winner and if you currently don't feel like you are winning in your life, I can help you move through the process.

Here are three habits that can move you forward so you can heal your heart and feel whole again.

1. Believe in the healing power of forgiveness. Forgive yourself. Forgive those who have harmed you. Let go of all attempts to change the past by holding onto it.
2. Honor yourself by saying 10-20 times a day, "I choose to open my heart to greater self-love."
3. Write down 100 ways that you are worthy. Read your words aloud for 100 days and feel the words as you read them.

One of my greatest joys in life is to help other people find their inner light. Contact me today to start your process at coachwinn@coachwinnspeaks.com and I will give you a FREE 50-minute discovery call to get you jumpstarted.

About the Author

Coach Sherry Winn is an in-demand motivational speaker, a leading success coach and seminar trainer, a two-time

Olympian, a national championship basketball coach, and an Amazon best seller. She has written five books including, *"Unleash the Winner within You: A Success Game Plan for Business, Leadership and Life."* Thousands, from small business owners to athletic coaches to corporate executives, have enjoyed Coach Winn's powerful interactive and humorous WINNING presentations.

With over 34 years of practicing leadership as an elite athlete and collegiate basketball coach, Sherry is an expert on coaching leaders and team members to championship status. She has successfully taken people beyond their levels of comfort to "WIN" against competitors who were superior in talent, facilities and financial budgets. Through her WIN Philosophy™ and WINNER Principles™, she teaches leaders and team members to be victorious even when the odds appear to be insurmountable.

A recognized authority on leadership and team development, Coach Winn shares with you the WINNER Principles which will enable you to rejuvenate, invigorate and stimulate you and your team members to become agents of change.

Audiences rave about Coach Winn's ability to enthusiastically deliver messages woven into humorous stories which are applicable for individuals within all levels of organizations. A passionate, sought-after author, speaker and business consultant, Coach Winn is characterized by friends, colleagues and clients as one of the most benevolent, perceptive and influential individuals in the business today.

Coach Winn is the originator of the WIN Philosophy ™ and the WINNER Principles ™, and is known for her passion and belief system that ALL things are possible.

Call or email Coach Winn for a media appearance, speaking or seminar engagements, or to inquire about her WINNING Coaching.

coachwinn@coachwinnspeaks.com
304-380-4398
www.facebook.com/coachwinnspeaks
www.linkedin.com/in/coachsherrywinn
www.twitter.com/coachwinnspeaks

THE STRENGTH OF YOUR STORY
By Jeanne Alford

You have a story. I have a story. Often, these stories don't reflect the full breadth of who we are and what we stand for in life. As a communications professional, I've seen this reflected in the stories we tell about ourselves, our businesses, our products and our services.

What I find fascinating, however, is how easy it can be to adjust these stories we tell. As a writer, we refer to it as editing. As a member of the human race, we lean on therapy. But I want to tell you a different way with a few distinct steps plus a little bit more.

I've worked with international brands and with esoteric, innovative start-ups. Throughout my career, I've trained world-renown executives to speak and introduced lifechanging technologies as well as managed breaking news.

Sounds exciting!

But, when I was caught up in the recent spate of downsizing, I found myself doubting my skills, my capabilities; dare I say?

My worth. Has that ever happened to you?

You know deep down who you are and what you can do, right? But amid this thing we call life, you get distracted or simply forget.

What's Your Story?

We tell stories.

Sometimes, these stories help us gain or regain our momentum. Sometimes, they stop us in our tracks. What story do you hear yourself telling every day?

I have three points I'd like to make regarding our personal and professional stories.

1. Be the author
2. Simply remember
3. Be confident

1. Be the Author

One of the toughest, but important, skills an author has is editing. I recall one of my college instructors telling me that you will write three pages before you even reach the beginning of your story. He was correct. We write our life story every day. We pull in stories from other sources. We get to edit, rewrite, reposition and rework every single one of them.

I recall speaking to a workshop leader recently. She was speaking to a group of women entrepreneurs about finance and investing. While chatting, she asked what I did. I told her I was writing an eBook on communications and her quick response was, "Oh, I'm not a writer." I started to question myself on why I was there! Instead I asked her what the most important message she had for this crowd of women. She said something about it's never too late to put a plan together. Then I asked if she had three main points to illustrate that message? Of course, she said. "You'll definitely hear them in my talk." I smiled and said, "Congratulations, you're a writer!" See, someone at some time in her past told her she could not string a sentence together. But that simply wasn't true. That story – that core belief – became an obstacle to her. She can now decide to edit that story or leave it. That's the power of being the author of your life.

I started using this "authoring and editing" technique a bit closer to home. When my son, a wonderfully gifted and intelligent young man, was in elementary school, he was very upset. He told me he was stupid. Apparently, according to him, his teacher told him so. Knowing his teacher, I was reasonably sure that was not the case. But I couldn't let that stand. We did an immediate "edit." I met with the teacher and my son. We discussed some issues my son had with reading. Apparently, one of his classmates told him he was stupid when he struggled with reading in front of the class. **With the teacher's help, we worked to redefine that story.** We also discovered he had a learning issue and got him the help he needed to overcome it. He reads fine today and no one would accuse him of being stupid. Can you imagine what a different life he would have lead if I didn't intervene and get him what he needed?

2. Simply Remember

So, you can now rethink some of those stories that seemingly drive your life, right? But, how do you start? I suggest you simply remember. Take some time to ponder who you are today. What little vignettes run through you mind? Where did you think, you would be five years ago and where are you in comparison? Did you reach your goals or did your goals change? Did you accomplish a few great milestones or do you think you've "missed the boat? What stories were you told that continue to define you today? Do you have stories like my son's "stupid story" where someone defined you? Were they correct or was this simply someone else's perspective? The important step in re-authoring your story and allowing yourself to bloom is to *simply remember*. **That is, to remember who you are at your very core.**

When I work with businesses, I ask them what their main marketing message is and how it compares with their competitors. We explore how they think their audiences view them. In addition, we identify those unique points that only they can offer – this is referred to as the Unique Selling Point or USP. I bring this up only to point out that this process is proven. By reminding these business clients about their origin, their audience and the intent for their product, we more easily define their specific marketing goals and messages.

Applying this knowledge to our own individual growth is done by simply remembering who we are.

How did you define yourself when you were a teen? In college? As a young adult? Did you find that your plans changed and you needed to be flexible? How did you grow when you found yourself faced with untenable challenges? Were you able to navigate through and see yourself in a new light? Did your focus change and did your passions alter?

Pondering these questions helps us to recognize and remember the essence of who we are. These memories –

or stories – provide a foundation for defining who we are today and help us to capture our own USP.

Now think a bit deeper. Did these memories come from your experience or were you given that information?

Why do I ask?

We are often told stories as we grow. From our families, our teachers, our friends. These stories come from their perspective, not yours. Early in my career, I had a supervisor who told me that I couldn't do something. I was devastated. I held such high esteem for this woman and I felt I let her down. It was a year or so later, when a new supervisor questioned me on why I wasn't completing certain tasks. When I told her this little anecdote, she sat me down for a long talk. **Basically, she explained that subconsciously I was using that story to stop my growth. She encouraged me to stretch and not be afraid to fail.** She instantly became my new mentor. I always had the skill, I just needed to refine my style. By changing that obstacle story, I changed the course of my career. That skill was news release writing and story pitching. That was more than 20 years ago; I built a successful career on that skillset.

So again, I suggest, take time to simply remember.

3. Be Confident

Now that we've discussed how we can edit our story to reauthor our lives and how remembering who we are is the key, let's discuss how to apply these to our daily lives. This step often proves to be tougher. That said, I have a perspective I'd like to share. **Just as the Viola Davis**

character in *The Help,* intoned: "You is kind. You is smart. You is important." I would add: *You is unique.*

Per the U.S. Bureau of Labor Statistics, there are more than 250,000 people that say that they can do what I do. That's a quarter of a million! Talk about stiff competition. But that number is not important. Why? I am unique.

Here's the point: You are unique. Take a moment and breathe that in.

Of all those hundreds of thousands of people who do what I do, not one of them had my mom and dad. Not one of them had my education. Not one of them had to do the kind of work that I did in my career to become who I am today. When I interviewed for my job at Dolby, there were probably 10 or 20 other people vying for that position. Because I had certain experiences and skills, I prevailed. **I'm proud of the work I did. Nobody else could have done it the way I did. That is also true for you.** Is there anybody out there that took every single class the same as you? I doubt that. Is there anybody else in your career path whose worked in the same companies, for the same amount of time, took the same workshops, had the same supervisors, managed the same teams, lived the same life? I don't think so.

These things make up who we are and what makes us unique. They make up the core of who we are and what we stand for. They give us the foundation to figure out who we want to be today and in the future. As much as we need to celebrate our successes, we need to celebrate our unique attributes! We need to stand strong in our uniqueness. Be confident that we are right where we are supposed to be.

Pulling It All Together

There is a secret to telling your story confidently. Marketing people know this as a basic truth. **You must tell it. Tell it often. Tell it consistently.** What does that mean to us in this context?

Only you can tell your story. Once you identify what is you versus what others have told you, you get to rewrite that story.

For example, my old boss told me I couldn't write. Working with a new mentor, I realized it was simply a style difference. I began writing more and honed that skill. Or my son heard that he was stupid – albeit from another child. Working with his teacher, we identified that was not true. He's grown into a highly intelligent young man.

This rewrite method helps in defining who you are today and who you will be in the future. It's useful in defining what you offer your friends, family, colleagues and clients. It's paramount in helping you recognize your own unique nature. By identifying those attributes, you can easily build your confidence.

Now when you tell your story again and again, you will grow stronger in its truth – that's where frequency comes in. Tell it consistently and it becomes even stronger. By consistency, I mean be mindful of your message. You may have different versions of your story to tell, as long as they have similar messages.

My recipe to bloom? Be the author of your life story, edit when necessary. Simply remember that you are the only person uniquely qualified to do what you do. Stay strong in knowing that your confidence is ultimately one of your strongest tools.

You have a story to tell. Only you can decide if it's the right story. I encourage you to choose your story wisely, share it frequently and SHINE!

About the Author

Jeanne Alford is an experienced speaker, trainer, writer and PR expert. She spent her career honing her expertise in communications. She has directed national and international public affairs and public relations programs for several brands including Dolby, Philips Electronics and Visa. She has also worked with leaders at some of the most innovative start-ups in Silicon Valley. No matter what position she held, her focus remains on telling the brand story.

In her career in PR and corporate communications, Jeanne's campaigns have changed media perceptions, garnered national and international awareness for issues and helped to strongly position executives as industry leaders. As an advocate for employee communications and crisis communications, she led programs to ensure that a company's most important asset, its people, are kept informed. As a trainer, she has assisted many executives in refining and leveraging their media efforts to ensure their company story is told through the eyes of respected media writers and broadcasters.

Today, Jeanne works with individuals and small businesses to tell their most compelling stories – in the media, with customers and among their colleagues. As a business and communications coach, she strives to apply those skills to help her clients tell their best stories using the most effective platforms. Her focus is on developing communications strategies and coaching business leaders to elevate and refine their message.

Jeanne has authored several business articles, white papers and marketing campaigns. Her materials have appeared in daily newspapers, national business publications and on several online sites. She most recently authored "3 Magic Questions to Instantly Improve Your Communications," which is available to download at BeClear101.com.

jeanne@alfordcommunications.com
Phone: 415-971-3344
www.alfordcommunications.com,
 www.beclear101.com
https://www.facebook.com/BeClear101-1896566077223594/
https://www.linkedin.com/in/jeannealford
Twitter: @jealford

AWAKEN TO EVERY MOMENT
By Holly Reese, MSOM, L.Ac.

Dawn slowly emerges from the darkness of night. It is during the night that I feel the most isolated and alone. The gradual brightening of my room is in stark contrast to the intolerable pain coursing through every cell in my body. I imagine the sun responds to my plea for help and moves faster. Afraid of igniting more pain, I cautiously turn my head towards the one window in my bedroom. I've grown quite attached to it. My unadorned, single-hung window is an indispensable lifeline that feeds me light and sound: my only connection to the world outside.

A ray of warm sunlight crawls through the window and makes it way towards my bed. It surprises me how much I need to know that the day is going to be warm and sunny. I hear the chirping of the birds that live in the tree outside my window. What I wouldn't give to be a bird right now, carefree and soaring through the skies with complete freedom. My only worry would be finding my next worm or bug to eat. Instead, for me, another day of despair begins. It's hard to believe that is my reality. Do you ever feel like you must be living in someone else's reality? This illness must be some kind of mistake. This can't be where I've been planted, can it?

By the summer of 2004, that's exactly how I felt. I found myself struggling to stay alive, while living in the basement bedroom of a friend's house. My life had come to a screeching halt two years earlier, when I developed a rare autoimmune illness. I spent the next twenty-four months sliding into the abyss of chronic illness. My muscles burned unceasingly, as if I was suspended in a vat of acid. The never-ending fatigue drained my life essence. I had barely enough energy to speak in a whisper. The connective tissue around the muscles in my body contracted and hardened until it felt as if I was wearing an unyielding suit of armor on the inside. It was difficult to breathe, let alone move. I lost the ability to digest solid food. My body atrophied, and every time I looked in the mirror, an emaciated skeleton stared back at me. Western medicine offered no hope and no cure. A Kaiser doctor told me that I should resign myself to "having bad days and worse days for the rest of my life."

What the heck happened? Who am I? What am I going to do now? I asked these questions on continuous replay. I felt so helpless. This was not at all how I envisioned my life would turn out. Ever since I was a little girl, I had always thought I had something important to do with my life. I had imagined I would grow up to be a renowned doctor, a visionary teacher, or a famous scientist. My work would be groundbreaking and better the lives of many people, especially women. So much for the big destiny I had envisioned for my life! If I remained as I was, immersed in a tar pit of suffering and incapable of even helping myself then my life was over. Have you ever felt trapped and hopeless?

Or in despair over not being where you thought you should be with your life?

On July 17th 2004, I had lost all hope of ever becoming well again. I could no longer bear living and attempted to end my life. Fortunately, I failed. At this pivotal moment, lying on my bed unable to move because of the pain and in despair over not even being able to end my own suffering, I gave up. And, I finally did what I should have done long before. I called out to Source for help and *I was answered*. There was a strong, visceral sensation in my heart chakra, as if it was actually vibrating. Through images, words, and emotions, I became aware of the guidance that Source had been transmitting all along. **The first message I received was that I had turned against myself and considered my own body as an enemy trying to kill me. Instead, I was directed to visualize the cells in my body as my family in need of love and support, not hate and anger.** That was a revelation! Until then, my thoughts were only on pain and suffering. My life seemed a failure. **I had been completely focused on what I didn't want.**

I was then instructed to begin my healing with a small step, to work on healing the pain in my hand. I was directed to use the color energies of the heart chakra, pink for love and green for healing. I placed all my awareness on my hand, sending it these vibrations. When I was finished, the searing agony in my right hand was gone. A casual observer might think that this was a small thing. But, for two years every cell in my body had felt as if it were on fire twenty-four-seven. Now, there was one part of my body that was experiencing absolutely no pain. It was a miracle! That experience saved my life and changed me forever. I thought that if I could be guided to create this tiny miracle of healing, what other things could I do? Could I not be well again?

That day of decision marked the beginning of my decade long holistic journey of recovery. Once I was no longer focused on everything I didn't want, the way was cleared for my connection to Source. I started paying attention to divine guidance and focused on hope and creation, rather than misery and suffering. Small miracles of attraction and healing began to occur every day. My full recovery was slow and progress was not always linear, but I did it. I used juicing to receive nutrition until my digestive system could handle solid food.

Then, I chose foods for medicinal purposes to speed my healing. I set and maintained my intentions for health by meditating and using visualizations. When, my inflammation receded and I could use my hands I was able to do acupuncture and reflexology. I practiced Medical Qigong and performed energy healing on myself. It was a journey of exploration and transformation.

Along the way, I discovered my true-life purpose. My passion is to teach women with a mission and a desire to make a positive impact on this world how to create and maintain, or regain vibrant health, holistically. All of the holistic techniques that I used to save my own life, I now teach others. **Looking back, I had perceived my illness as a failure or worse – a punishment, but nothing could be further from the truth. I didn't know it at the time, but I was learning how to bloom where I was planted.** What does bloom where you are planted and discover how to (Shine) mean to me? As I progressed along my path to wellness, I became adept at **using the power of Now to**

attract what I needed to take my next step. Often, in my case, that was literal. This is the act of Blooming where you are planted. Before I experienced my spiritual epiphany on that critical day of decision, I was defined by the limitations of my illness. I was tied to what I had created in the past and unable to move forward.

The ability to Bloom where I was planted led me from one healing moment and technique to the next. Blooming takes you past the obstacles constructed in the past by using the present moment, which offers us unlimited potential for creation. **Blooming is a skill that can be learned, as is the ability to Shine.** Before my illness, if asked, I would have equated Shining with perhaps a successful career, health, wealth, and a loving partner. But, these are all things that can be achieved, acquired, or attracted. Being asked that question now, my answer is completely different. **Shining is a state of being; it comes from within. It means to operate from your higher self, the part of you that resides in the heart chakra and is connected to Source.** Use that connection to move through life discovering and fulfilling your life purpose, and you will shine. You can shine anytime, anywhere, and anyplace you are, right now.

What can you do right now to learn how to Bloom where you are and Shine?

Step 1: Connect to the Now and Clear the Clutter

You can learn to do this through abdominal breathing. Breathe deeply drawing the air in and all the way down to your navel. Breathe in life and healing energy, draw it down to your navel, which is your center of power, and hold it for a few seconds. Then, exhale fully and completely, allowing all that no longer serves you to flow out. Let go of stress, worry, and concerns. Your only focus is your breath and letting go. Do this for 5 breaths. This will clear your clutter and begin to focus your awareness on the now.

Step 2: Open to Receive Guidance from Source

During the next 5 breaths, continue to breathe deeply down to your navel. Center your awareness within your heart chakra.

Activate your higher self by intention. Simply call to it in your mind. Then, with every breath focus on your intention of easily receiving guidance from Source for your highest good.

Step 3: Use the Power of the Moment to Attract your next Step

The next five breaths are used to ask for the guidance you need to discover and take your next step. Focus on it and visualize that it is already done. Feel that it is done; know that it is done, and feel gratitude for your accomplishment. You may now go on about your day. Be aware of what is going on all around you and you will receive the guidance you asked for. Source will use many methods to guide you, your only job is to be aware enough to see, hear, feel, or know it when it appears.

Step 4: Discover Your Shine

The clearer and focused you are on what you want and who you want to be, the faster Source can help you to Shine. Set aside some time to get to know yourself. Purchase a journal and explore these questions. What do you like to do? Who would you like to be? What are you doing now that you like, or don't like? Create and describe your grandest vision for yourself and don't hold back with your dreams and passions. Self-creation is fun! You can be or do anything. As you become clear on how you want to shine, focus on this with hope and excitement, I guarantee that the tools, tips, guidance, people, and experiences that you need will present themselves. Remain aware of all that is around you. Every day, reflect on what you did, saw, heard, or experienced. Identify all that exemplifies how you want to shine. Recognize it. Acknowledge it with gratitude. Thank Source, and ask for more! Your job is to be aware and open enough to recognize the treasures you are receiving to help you become your grandest vision of yourself.

"That is the real spiritual awakening, when something emerges from within you that is deeper than who you thought you were. So, the person is still there, but one could almost say that something more powerful shines through the person. You are here to enable the divine purpose of the universe to unfold. That is how important you are!" Eckhart Tolle

About the Author

Holly has a master's degree in Oriental medicine, (MSOM), and is a California board-licensed acupuncturist, (L.Ac.), and herbalist. In addition, she also holds certifications in Medical Qigong, acupressure, hypnotherapy, and past life regression.

Also, as a certified personal trainer and martial arts instructor, Holly has rigorously studied kinesiology, qi, energy work, and meditation for more than thirty years. She holds two black belts, one in Tae Kwon Do and the other in Choy Lay Fut Kung Fu. Having graduated from MIT with a Bachelor of Science in electrical engineering, she also worked as a highly successful computer programmer for ten years before following her heart to work in the holistic health field.

Holly lives in her beloved San Francisco Bay Area and has a successful practice as a Holistic Heath Coach. She teaches holistic wellness classes, regularly speaks at events and has published a gripping and empowering memoir called: "Rising from the Abyss: My Journey into and out of Chronic Illness." It chronicles her decade long journey back to health from a rare and nearly fatal autoimmune illness called mixed connective tissue disorder using holistic methods.

Holly's passion is to teach women leaders – women with a mission - how to create and maintain or regain vibrant health using holistic methods. She offers various private and group coaching programs to ignite your vitality and be the role model you want to be!

Email: holly@hollyreeselac.com

Phone: (510) 484-4253

Websites: www.inspirewellnesscenter.com
www.hollyreeselac.com

Facebook: www.facebook.com/InspireWellnessCenter

LinkedIn: https://www.linkedin.com/in/holly-reeseholistichealth

Twitter: www.twitter.com/HollyReeseLAc

Section 3
DISCOVER YOUR BEAUTY, GIFTS, TALENTS AND ABILITIES.

You are beautifully, uniquely, and wonderfully made. Gain tips, tools and practices to help you discover the wonder of you and SHINE!

DRIVEN TO THRIVE
By Samantha Jansen

"Be Yourself, Chase those Dreams and Believe in Yourself"

--- Samantha Jansen

No matter what stage you are in your life right now, we have all experienced setbacks, challenges and sometimes life changing situations. Often these situations create an anchor; which results in attaching a feeling or an emotion to specific situations or environments. This over time can lead into stress and/or anxiety.

I have personally been through this and witness countless individuals go through this experience. I speak to people every day and at least a few times a week I hear their pain, anxiety and fear in their voices. No matter their household role, business status, financial situation, countless women and men experience similar situations.

About six years ago, I embarked on a journey like nothing I have ever done before. I walked away from a secure high paying corporate job to embark on a journey to fulfil myself. I made the decision to start a business.

The decision was driven by emotions of excitement and fear, the potential to fulfil my purpose and passion, and finally having the courage to learn the lessons after months and months of setbacks, and challenges in my personal life with my partner at the time. I was a single mum parenting a threeyear-old, pregnant and living the crazy 9 –5 rat race of juggling a job to sustain a lifestyle I didn't really want to keep pursuing. I lived in a beautiful home, had money to get by each day, bills were paid, but something was missing. The more I thought about it, the more curious I became about finding a way to live a fulfilled life.

Upon reflecting back, I have often wondered why I didn't make a conscious decision to self-discovery and pursue my purpose sooner. However, over the years of investing in countless selfdevelopment books and programs, working with life coaches, and business coaches, I have discovered it's all about the timing, being in sync and alignment to yourself in every aspect.

> The moment I understood this, I felt a sense of accomplishment.

(A BIG, Ah Ha moment for me, I have been learning, reflecting and implementing ever since.) It's been hard work and challenging, yet rewarding in so many ways.

The Journey of Transformation

I had a great high paying job working for a well-established financial services company in the heart of Melbourne, Australia. I was a single mum with a baby on the way and I knew I couldn't physically keep up the rat race. I would get home from work around 6pm every day as I commuted to work on the train and I would spend about an hour or so with my three-year-old before I would tuck her into bed and read a bedtime story to her each night.

The more I thought about this life style I was living, the more I started to question the world around me. It made me think about other people who might be experiencing something similar. Often we don't think about how many others might be experiencing the same thing. How many parents might be living like this? Is there a better way? How does one transition from a hectic life that isn't fulfilling to living life on their terms?

What is the transitional process really like? The above questions played on my mind day after day as I juggled it all, keep a straight face to the outside world, being pregnant and raising a three-year-old on my own. The journey to finding my purpose wasn't the hard part, it was overcoming the negativity, objections and critics from society that was the most challenging for me.

A letter from me to you

Dear _____,

If you often struggle with overwhelm and stress of trying to do it all. I hear you. I have been there too. I know it feels like a long dark road with small lights appearing once in a while. I have walked that road too.

I have often wondered why we put so much pressure on ourselves. Why do we pay attention to all that people have to say? The truth is as humans we seek love and acceptance. We want to be heard and seen. This often results in listening and paying attention to everyone's comments about our needs. When really it's about **"what's best for you"**

When we decide to pursue something for ourselves, we are consumed by guilt. Over the years of learning and investing into personal development; I have discovered how to get rid of guilt and you can too. Guilt doesn't have to be an indication of you pursuing your dreams, career or running a business particularly if you are raising a family.

The truth is that you can enjoy both Life and Business, raise a family, pursuing a career all at the same time. It's about creating your perfect lifestyle and not worrying about external judgment. I strongly encourage you to chase those dreams, set yourself BIG goals and start taking action.

Love,
Samantha x

Overcoming Objections and Challenges

For as long as I can reminder, well into my childhood years. I have always seen an objection as a challenge I must win. I am a little competitive and enjoying challenging myself. I thrive on setting BIG scary and audacious goals; they are my drivers in life. I was born and educated in Colombo, Srilanka, before migrating to Melbourne, Australian in 2004.

My parents divorced when I was about 10 years ago and my mum raised my brother and myself fulltime. I learned a lot from her, as a young child growing up; I paid attention to the world around me. Back in the 1995 in Sri Lanka divorcing wasn't socially accepted and mostly frowned upon. However, my mum didn't let society get the better of her when my dad left her. She took time to grieve and surround herself with people who loved and supported her. This made a massive difference to her emotional wellbeing and us growing up as teenagers and young adults.

The learning I witnessed growing up helped me become a strong confident woman. People often say to me to me that I have experienced a lot of challenges throughout my childhood and adult life. As I might have attracted some of these things too. However, I see the world differently.

"I'm not a victim to any of these situations, I'm an achiever who learned lessons and experienced life"

As humans, it's easy to get caught up life's challenges and feel like a victim. Some experiences are harder than others. The emotional pain can consume us to breaking point. I have felt that pain. I have cried myself to sleep for days, weeks and months, when my partner walked out leaving me to raise a three-year old, while being six months pregnant and having to figure it all out. Every morning I would wake up and think

"What's my mission today?"

I wasn't depressed, I was sad and confused. I wasn't sure how to move forward as a mum. Why? Because my thinking about what's best for the kids. I wasn't really thinking about the BIG picture and the future as I was consumed by living in past emotions and present with no clarity. I wanted answers, I wanted clarity, but I didn't know where to start. The moment I decided to start looking at myself from within and focus on me. My life started to change. My focus had shifted and my conscious mind and subconscious mind were starting to work in sync to some extent and I was starting see a glimpse of clarity.

Stimulating the Mind, Body and Soul

After months and months of uncurtaining I made the transition. I shifted my focus and I decided to focus on myself. This decision was aided by investing in meditation, yoga, me time, reading books and investing in support (mentors, coaches and programs)

It was slightly challenging to be honest. I was a mum on maternity leave with limited financial resource and risking a lot to explore a new way of life. I did feel a little sick in my tummy the first time I paid for my first business coach and then a life coach too.

The moment I made the decision to invest in myself and take the time to really find my purpose in life, map out my values and mission. I was then up against society judging me and making comments about me trying to chase my dreams when I should be focusing on parenting a new born and toddler instead of investing money in courses and trying to start a business.

Sometimes their comments made me emotional, however using my new-found techniques, I was able to quickly move past the negativity and look for a lesson. I could learn from their comments. The challenge was to overcome and within a few months of being on maternity leave, juggling a new born and parenting a three-year-old I launched a business.

A business driven by my passion and aligned with my purpose. It was all starting to fall into place one step at a time. I took the time to plan the business strategically; I wanted a lifestyle business with freedom. A business that gave me a passive income, freedom to travel, enjoys motherhood and life. All the while, serving my clients.

The more I invested in myself and gave myself time to reflect and learn, the more success I experienced. I eliminated the guilt for not wanting to be a full-time mum. When I'm home with the kids, I'm present with them. We would spend quality time together, watch movies, read books and create memories together.

Since launching the business, my life has been filled with a heartfelt feeling of love and sense of accomplishment. When I'm working, talking to clients, running events and workshops or even traveling. It's about me helping others succeed and sharing my knowledge. It's rewarding and fun.

Heartfelt Desires

Have you taken the time to discover what your heart and soul desires?

- Do you love to travel and explore beautiful cities?
- Do you want to start a business?
- Have you thought about what makes you really happy? Often this leads into your passion and flows into your personal purpose.
- What do you want to achieve by your next milestone birthday?
- Are seeking to build financial freedom and live your ideal lifestyle?

It's really important to take the time to self-reflect and look around your surroundings. Surround yourself with the right people, seek support, invest in mentors and programs, read books and most importantly take action.

"Your success to thrive is depended on you level of commitment to take action".

Choose an environment filled with love, happiness and encouragement. Surround yourself with people who want to hear your dreams and goals. People who see your BIG vision and encourage you to go out there achieve it and make a difference. Time isn't replaceable. Make those decisions and take action. Your personal purpose, self-driven patterns will unleash your potential to thrive. Be open to opportunity and explore your surroundings.

About the Author

Samantha Jansen is the founder of Platform 4 Success and Samantha Jansen Publishing, An International Speaker, Author and Self Confessed Social Media Lover. Samantha Jansen is on a mission to help small business owners build an influential profile and highly profitable businesses. As a selfconfession lover of social media, she helps business owners understand the power of social media in today's marketing world along with harnessing the power in selfpublishing. She says, "Self-Publishing and Social Media Marketing is one of the most powerful ways to fast track your business and build an influential profile".

She has co-authored 5 anthologies which include "Rebook Your Life" alongside Dr. John Demartini. She has also written her own book **"No Qualifications, No Excuses - How to build a business even when the odds are against you",** When Samantha isn't consulting clients and running workshops, she is out networking with local business owners, all this while being a mum to Sierra and Savinesh.

+61430 022 762
Samantha@platform4success.com
www.platform4success.com
 www.samanthajansen.com.au
facebook.com/Platform4Success
facebook.com/TheAuthorSamanthaJansen/
Twitter @JansenSammy

BLOOM WHEN LIFE FALLS APART
By Nancy Monson

My legs gave out and I collapsed on my friend's kitchen floor when I heard the words I couldn't believe. He didn't want to work things out; he wanted a divorce. I felt all the energy drain out of my body, and I started sobbing. I pleaded with my husband to give us a chance. I offered to come back to Iowa and work things out. It didn't matter; he was resolute. He said even if I returned, he would not try again. He was done.

I hung up the phone and staggered to my feet, tears streaming down my cheeks and legs weak and wobbly. I couldn't believe what was happening. I was only back in California a week and my entire world was crumbling. I ached inside. I felt lost, overwhelmed and hopeless.

A year before, my husband and I had excitedly moved to Iowa so I could attend the Transcendental Meditation university. He had attended before I met him. It was his suggestion that I apply for their one-year master's program to study the ancient Vedic knowledge of meditation and enlightenment— something he knew and I deeply yearned to explore.

We packed up our home in Phoenix and together with my cat, headed to Fairfield, the small town in rural Iowa where thousands of Transcendental Meditation practitioners lived and meditated. I was thrilled to finally, after so many years of seeking, be submersing myself in sacred wisdom and transformative practice.

But our year in Fairfield was very difficult for our young marriage. We were only married a few months when we moved to Fairfield, and during our time there, we struggled. We found ourselves frequently in conflict that somehow we were unable to resolve. My master's program was intense and took up practically all my time. Money was extremely tight, adding to our growing stress as my husband struggled to find work to support us while I was in school. He left a fruitful consulting business in Phoenix, and returning to Iowa, found it very difficult to secure work.

In the spring, I learned that my mother was losing her battle with Parkinson's; I knew deep in my heart that she would not live much longer. I longed to return to California to help care for her and share her remaining days. My husband did not want to move to California; he was happy living in Iowa. We strained to find a resolution that would work for both of us. Our solution emerged after many difficult and tearful conversations. We agreed that I would complete my masters and return to California to be with my mother. We would do our best to have a long-distance marriage for the remaining time my mother was alive.

That was the plan. Unfortunately, after all we had been through, he was done. I was now left to carry on alone. It was a very dark time for me. The man I had committed my heart to was asking to end our brief marriage. My mother was dying.

My part-time job did not pay enough to cover my expenses. My cat—my solace through so many challenges in my life—developed debilitating glaucoma. I was $40,000 in debt from student loans, a car loan, and credit card balances that had accumulated from our money struggles. I had only my personal belongings as everything else I left behind in Iowa, thinking I would not be in California very long. I didn't even have a bed in the very empty, tiny apartment I rented.

My first year back in California was fraught with navigating all that I faced; I succumbed to another bout of depression. My saving grace was my meditation practice, my bicycle, my beloved kitty, and my best friend who I had met in school in Iowa. She was also going through a traumatic divorce, and we made a pact that we would not "check out" on each other during our struggles. Without that promise, I'm not sure I would have survived that first year. But slowly, one step at a time, I climbed out of the dark pit of my depression and grief from my mother's drastic decline and the love and life I lost.

A year after returning to California, I was introduced to the growing profession of life coaching. Incredibly curious, I signed up for the introductory workshop. Thrilled with what I learned in the first class, I knew that I wanted to complete the entire training program. That was a turning point for me. I had found something that engaged, energized and inspired me!

Two months into my coach training, a friend introduced me to the CEO of a small boutique executive coaching firm. He was looking to bring onboard someone with organization change experience, and after learning of my tenure as a change management consultant with the reputable consulting firm Accenture, he was anxious for me to join his team. Not only did he want me to build their reputation in organization change consulting, but he offered to help me become an executive coach for their firm. I was ecstatic! I was finally emerging out of the bleakness I had been navigating since leaving Iowa.

Having to build a new life out of the ashes of despair was one of the most difficult situations I've ever faced. Being hit with so many challenges threw me into the pit of depression again, but I didn't "check out." I chose to persevere and take the steps—one by one—to take care of myself and reinvent my life. It wasn't easy, and there were times where I almost gave up. Slowly with help, I recovered and rebuilt.

Three years after my divorce, my only remaining debt was my student loan. I had furnished my apartment, built a successful reputation as an executive coach, and was in a loving relationship. Out of that rocky ground, I learned how to bloom where I had been planted and create a life I loved.

It is not easy to find the strength and courage when life deals us such intense blows. Sometimes we feel as if life is against us and gives us much more than we can manage. I know. I was there many times during the year after Iowa, but I kept going—with support. The result is that I am a stronger, more confident woman who creates her own life on her terms. I didn't give up, and I want to encourage you to never give up.

You too can bloom and shine!

If you feel you've been dealt a terrific blow of difficult circumstances in your life I offer the following tips that not only have helped me, but have helped the many women I have assisted since becoming a life and executive coach sixteen years ago.

Tips to Building a Life You Love:

1. Reach out and get support.

We are not meant to handle life alone, and it's particularly important in challenging times. Close friends and family who accept you and encourage you are invaluable. If my friend was not there, I'm not sure I would have survived that year. There were many times in my dark depression that I called sobbing, and she comforted, listened and talked me through.

The important thing is that your friend or family member will be there for you when you need their ear and heart during those dark moments of despair. It's also essential to have the support of a coach, therapist or spiritual guide to help you navigate such a challenging time and guide you through the fog of overwhelm and depression that can cloud your thinking and dampen your faith in a more uplifting future.

2. Get outside and move your body.

During my year, I committed to staying active. I love riding my bike and hiking, and I made sure I was outside either riding or hiking at every opportunity, particularly when it was sunny. Being outside and moving is one of the best ways to treat depression and overwhelm. Getting out in the fresh air, seeing the beauty of nature and moving your body will help shift your perspective, expand your vision and reinvigorate your spirit. Even a ten minute daily walk outside can do wonders for your heart and soul.

3. **Incorporate meditation or some type of mindful practice.**

There are mountains of research on the reduction of stress and restorative benefits of a meditative or mindfulness practice. This was my saving grace during my year. All that I learned and experienced in my masters' program I put to use and consistently meditated, even if only a short time, every day. I know that it helped me survive the many rocky days and nights I endured.

Today when I work with my clients, one of the very first things we do is establish a morning meditative practice. Even five minutes of focusing on one's breath done regularly can make a huge difference. Joining a meditation group, listening to guided meditations, incorporating daily prayer or gratitude practice, and performing yoga are a few ways you can start to incorporate this supportive benefit.

4. **Keep a journal.**

I have kept a journal for twenty years, and during the year of rebuilding my life, I wrote every single day, even if it was just a brief entry. As the months went by, my journal helped me to remember how far I'd come as I went back to read earlier entries. Those pages gave me confidence and faith that I would regain my love of life. A simple practice of writing nonstop for five to ten minutes each morning can help you clear out and move through all that you are dealing with.

If you've never kept a journal, here's a way to start. Buy a beautiful journal and a pen you love and commit to writing for five minutes every morning for one week. Just write and don't edit, filter or stop. No matter what comes up, keep writing, even if it makes no sense. You're building a practice. When you are comfortable, add more minutes.

5. Make self-care non-negotiable.

When we feel lost, abandoned, overwhelmed, depressed, alone or weary from the challenges of our lives, the best thing we can do for ourselves is to nourish and comfort our bodies and hearts. My heart was hurting, and I was exhausted from life's many blows.

Buying myself fresh flowers, letting myself sleep extra hours, luxuriating in restorative baths, taking myself to a movie, and preparing a yummy healthy meal were some of the ways I nourished myself. During difficult times, it's common for self-care to go out the window in favor of working harder, numbing out with unhealthy habits, or just keep pushing ahead. It's during these rocky times that self-care is most important and beneficial. Start by committing one night a week to treating yourself to something that nourishes your heart and body.

6. Explore what brings you joy.

When I learned about life coaching, I followed my curiosity and signed up for an introductory workshop. Had I not followed my interest, I may never have discovered the joy and fulfillment I experience today as a life and executive coach. A key step in any major life transition is to give yourself permission to explore what ignites your curiosity or brings you joy.

The key is to explore without commitment until you are clear that you're ready to take the plunge and dive in. It was during the introduction to coaching workshop that I became 100% clear I wanted to be a coach. I needed to put my toe in the water and test before I committed to the entire training and eventual certification program. During any major transition or time of challenge, it is just as critical to start exploring what brings you joy as it is to support yourself with the tips I outline above. Give yourself permission to take classes, go on trips, try out new hobbies that you've longed to investigate if you feel the energy and excitement to do so. See where it might take you. It could be the start of your new life!

You will bloom again if you commit to making the journey in a way that supports your heart, body and soul. I know. I emerged from my dark year more vibrant and stronger with a more fulfilling life than before. Yes, there was loss…a lot of it, but the loss opened the way for new life. A new life that I love. Today, I am enjoying my life as it continues to unfold in magical ways from the plowing of the field of my old life.

If this story has touched you, I have a gift for you! Over my many years as a life coach and spiritual guide, I have learned there is a deeper process and purpose to these dramatic changes in our lives. To help you understand what's unfolding at a deeper level within your being, I offer my eBook, *When Life Falls Apart,* to support you through tough times. You will find the link to download your free copy in my bio that follows. It's my gift to you to help you gently navigate challenging life passages. We are not meant to face difficult times alone or without a guide. I hope the tips above and my free eBook help you bloom right where you are planted and SHINE!

About the Author

Nancy Monson, founder of Everyday Spirituality, is a Soul Purpose Advocate devoted to helping people live their soul's greatest expression every day. She brings a multitude of skills, talents, wisdom and a lifetime of transformative experiences to guide people who are truly ready to live their soul's potential and purpose every day.

Working in both corporate consulting and personal transformation for the past twenty years, Nancy has a rare combination of experience helping hundreds of senior leaders, executive teams, and entrepreneurs using her unique combination of strategic, intuitive and pragmatic skills. This experience gives her a special ability to mentor women leaders and entrepreneurs as they struggle to navigate their own personal transformations. Her greatest fulfillment comes from confidently guiding women dealing with difficult and challenging life changes to create truly powerful, authentic soul-directed lives.

Nancy holds an MBA in Organizational Behavior from UC Berkeley's Hass School of Business, an MA in the Science of Creative Intelligence from the Maharishi University of Management, and a BS in Mathematics from Cal Poly, San Luis Obispo. She also has completed numerous trainings with special emphasis in Human Design, Gene Keys, Evolutionary Leadership, life and relationship coaching, spiritual guidance, Tantric counseling, Deep Emotional Release™ bodywork, and Reiki energy healing. Nancy is also a facilitator of 7 Habits of Highly Effective People personal empowerment course, and a coach of the Women, Power, and Body Esteem transformation program for women.

Nancy is also an adventurer. She treasures the outdoors, and spends as much time as she can be hiking the hills around her California home. In her years of travel and outdoor adventure, she has hiked the Sierra Nevada, the Cascades, Andes, Himalayas, Alaska Range, Brooks Range, and the Rockies. She has backpacked one range or another during every season of the year, climbed frozen waterfalls, numerous rock faces and mountains, and camped on snowy glaciers. Her greatest accomplishment was climbing Denali, the highest peak in North America at the time when it was uncommon to see women in such sports. She believes nature is immensely healing and transformative, taking us to a deep place of inner connection with our own true nature.

Her gift to you is her eBook, *When Life Falls Apart*. You can download your free copy using this link:

http://everydayspirituality.com/whenlifefallsapart/
nancy@everydayspirituality.com
209.217.8120
www.EverydaySpirituality.com
https://www.facebook.com/nlmonson
https://www.linkedin.com/in/nancymonson
https://twitter.com/Nancyne

LIVE TO LOVE
By Fariba Haidari

People say the eyes are the windows to the soul. I believe this statement couldn't be more true.

As a child, I often wondered "Do these people know what I go through every day?" I wanted to cry and just spill the beans. Something always stopped me. Fear of what would happen if they found out. What would they think? What would they do? What would happen to me? What would happen to my sisters? What would happen to my mom? These were daily questions that I would ask myself in addition to why? Questions a little girl should not be asking. My child eyes reflected deep sadness, fear, and a lack of trust.

The pain I felt was not only extremely physical but very emotional. Not a day passed that I didn't question my very existence. I would beg God to end my life. Wishes a little girl should not be wishing.

At a young age, I was fascinated with analyzing people, beginning with my mother. I wanted to figure her out. What was the reason for her madness? Was it my fault? There had to be a reason. I knew that her excuse of blaming my sisters and I was not true. I would soon realize that her mental illness was far beyond anything I was capable of analyzing much less repairing.

I felt like the chosen one to protect my sisters. Literally becoming a shield at times. I felt so helpless because I did not know what the right thing to do was.

This was my experience for the first 14 years of my life.

At some point the school faculty began to get very suspicious. They had a meeting with me regarding several bruises and marks that they had observed on my hands and face. Naturally, I denied everything and made an excuse for what the bruises were caused by. Eventually running out of excuses. They disclosed to me that they are trained in detecting child abuse and they believe that I am a victim.

A part of me deep down inside just wanted to cry and tell them everything and just hug them. Then there was the other part of me that said no they're going to take you away, separate your sisters and put your mom in jail. I never wanted that to happen. This was my family…I didn't want to turn them in or abandon them. Eventually the school had a conference with me and told me that they are going to contact Child Protective Services with their concerns.

At this point I was completely scared and ask them to give me one weeks to find a close relative that would be willing to rescue my sisters and I together. After some thought they considered my proposal and give me one weeks' time. I contacted my uncle and shared with him what had happened and what was going to occur if someone wouldn't help us. He was a very busy man and had several big responsibilities in his life and suggested that I contact my father, whom I didn't even know was alive. My mother had said that he had been killed in the war. So, he asked me to call back the next day and he would provide me with a phone number.

Next day couldn't come any soon enough! I was up all night thinking of how I was going to introduce myself to him. During my school lunch, I used the payphone and called him. I said "Hi this is Fariba, I am your daughter." It was so silent on the phone you can hear a pin drop in another room. Then I just continued "I'm your oldest daughter from your previous wife." I still heard nothing back I thought maybe we got disconnected. As I took a deep breath to try to reintroduce myself again, I heard him excitedly say "Oh, how are you? How is your mom? Your sisters?" After telling him how we are and where we live and everything, I told him the purpose of my call. I didn't know what to expect and I was ready to accept anything that he was going to say.

After hearing, what had happened he reassured me that he knows her personality and she does have some to sort of mental disorder and it's not our fault. For the first time in my life I felt like somebody knew what I was talking about. My lunchtime was soon over, I quickly added that he should rescue us before they place us in Foster care. We had very little time. He said he was going to be there in one week to pick us up.

That entire week I was so nervous. What if my mom would find out? What would she do to me? She would kill me! That entire time I may have slept only a few hours every night, and that with nightmares. I couldn't even tell my sisters about all these things because they were younger and I was afraid they were going to accidentally say something. They attended a different school than I. My school faculty had informed their school as well, of the events unfolding. Finally, the day and time was set for the transition.

I remember attending each of my classes that day anticipating the moment that I would actually meet him. It felt like a very long time but sometime late morning they called me to the office. I walked into the conference room and there they were. People from the Child Protective Services, my school staff, the principal, vice principal, some teachers and the man I instantly knew, was my father. He opened his arms and embraced me so tightly that I still remember the smell of leather jacket.

After taking care of some technical things, we proceeded to go to my sisters' school and rescued them too. Coincidentally the next day with my 14th birthday. We were living in Virginia at the time and my father was living in California. His close friends had found out that he was in the area and invited us all to celebrate my birthday! My father took us all shopping the next day. We were so excited and relieved that we were out of that abusive environment finally.

He then proceeded to bring us to California after visiting a couple of more relatives on the way. When we arrived, we had no idea the worst was yet to come. Until then, we were only familiar with physical and emotional abuse we didn't know other kinds existed. To escape these horrible circumstances, I got married at 14 and had my first child at 15. I divorced when I was 18. My helpless sisters had their own painful journeys.

The saying goes what doesn't break you makes you stronger. My sisters and I are some of the strongest people in the world. If a human being can survive the things that we have, this is proof that we can achieve anything.

If success was measured by your gratification and satisfaction that you have received in life, then I feel as if I am the richest person on earth.

About 15 years ago due to life circumstances and many negative things occurring simultaneously I decided to give up on life. I had decided that death, was the only answer. I made out a will and wrote a letter to my family apologizing and expressing my love for everyone. The plan was that I was going to wait for my father to go to sleep and I was going to go jump off of the bridge. As I lay there and made 100% commitment to this, I somehow had a vision.

The Vision

I saw myself on the second story of a warehouse that was very high. I was sitting there packing my suitcase with a friend and suddenly the cement ground gave way. As the ground crumbled, her and we began to fall…falling all the way toward the first floor. As we were falling, I looked at her and I said "I will see you on the other side" because I knew that we were going to die. As my head impacted the cement floor I literally felt every bone in my body shatter like glass. It's hard to imagine how that feels but I actually felt every single bone in my body shatter.

Shortly after I saw all the light around me reduced to a dot. Within seconds that dot disappeared as well. The feeling I had I will never forget. There are no words to describe the fear that I had. Imagine complete hopelessness, complete void, darkness, terror, all horrible feelings and one. It was at that second that I realized that I had made a big mistake.

I just remember screaming for help and asking God for forgiveness. Shortly after, I was sitting up and I could not stop crying for the next 2 1/2 hours. After that I was so thankful to be alive I couldn't believe how underrated death was and I couldn't believe that God had given me a chance. I felt so much love from God, realizing that he allowed me to experience such a feeling before I would've made the biggest mistake of my life.

After this day, I became very optimistic. My eyes start to reflect joy, hope, warmth, and love. I got a great job, got back on my own feet and doors began to open because I knew whatever the circumstances in my life, would be much better than death.

A few years ago, I met Rebecca Hall Gruyter, a blessing in disguise. She had been interested in manufacturing her CD/DVD sets of her programs. Found the company I was working for and called to place an order. I was her account manager and we met. We had such a great time, laughing and talking we nearly forgot the CD order! I added her on Facebook to stay in touch. Sometime later, she posted on Facebook needing a recommendation for a sound engineer for her events. I responded and offered my services. We came to an agreement and I was soon her "Audio Wizard"

She had briefed me on the types of events she holds. I had no idea what the universe was aligning me for. The beautiful stories that I heard were so heart touching I listened, I cried & I laughed as I sat there behind my sound board. Observing and absorbing everything. I feel so blessed to have met so many incredibly inspirational people with such beautiful vibes & messages. A nourishment my soul was in dire need for, due to all of the emotional and physical pain that I had suffered. Now, I'm part of a community that nourishes me, inspires me, and lifts me. It has helped me fall in love with myself.

Imagine if the happiness, excitement & optimism that you feel when you are in love, can be duplicated in everyday life. It can, if you first fall in love with yourself. Often times we don't realize that we can do that. Try it, you will be pleasantly surprised. Give yourself a hug, treat yourself to a great dinner, nice perfume, a vacation and everything in between! Love yourself, you are the only you out there. You are special, unique, beautiful, brilliant and alive! Never give up!

How would you treat others if you knew today was your last day?

How would you treat others if you knew today was their last day?

Forgiveness releases you from the pain. This statement didn't make sense to me for many years. However, when you really think about it's very true. You see the person that has hurt you has hurt you and moved on but if you're going to constantly think about it and have that negative vibration of energy, that fiction is causing you to suffer.

However, by releasing that and just forgiving and leaving it be, you are releasing the vibration of negative energy. And that's when you're able to forgive and live in peace.

It's easier said than done. It may take time for some but it's wonderful when it happens. You feel a sense of freedom and empowerment because that negative feeling in memory no longer controls you. You have now controlled it.

(Remember, this starts with learning to love yourself)

Why are you here? Discover your why because you are a beautiful gift absolutely needed in this world.

Find a community to nourish, inspire and build you up. I was hesitant to pursue this project of sharing my experience and not having a success story at the end but I as I thought about it further. I realized that I am the success story. I am here and I'm alive. If I can inspire anyone or touch anyone's heart, I know I am achieving part of my "why". In daily life, it natural to lose focus of our "why" but it's opportunities like this that remind us. And remember…. Never give up!!

About the Author

Mother, Writer, Singer and entrepreneur with a BA in Business Management, Fariba Haidari, a San Francisco Bay Area resident with a Unique Power of Combining Logic & Creativity to produce Genius!

Her business acumen, technical expertise & leadership capabilities have contributed to a number of successful projects. Some of her current assignments include Writing, Singing, Event/Stage Management, Sound Engineering, Harmonium Restorer & Tuning Expert, co-author of an upcoming book with a degree in Business Management to name a few.

Fariba has a humanitarian philosophy which has enabled her to be a patient listener, that enjoys sharing knowledge, advice, hope, inspiration & even material possessions to those who solicit help or emotional support.

Despite Her life experiences, she can still see the glass half full and she continues to fulfill her ambitions against all odds.

Feel free to reach out to her at any of the following:

Email: faribahaidari@yahoo.com
Phone: 510-688-2524
Facebook: Fariba Haidari
Facebook fan page
@faribahaidarimusic
Snapchat: fariba_and_farial
Instagram: fariba_and_farial
Linkedin: http://linkedin.com/in/fariba-haidari-1255635a
YouTube: https://www.youtube.com/user/faribaandfarial
Twitter: @faribahaidari

UNLEASH...COME HOME TO YOU
By Mary E. Knippel

When I was 8-years-old I used to stand on a beautiful stage and (wow) my audiences with my performances. Every ear eagerly longed to hear, what I was going to say next. Of course, my stage was a giant boulder at the edge of a grove of trees and I was facing a field full of corn ready to be harvested. I knew I was going to be interviewed some day and I would be prepared, even if no one else in my world thought it would ever happen to me.

Just keep coming home to yourself for you are the one, who you've been waiting for. -Byron Katie

Fast forward to today where I have had some amazing opportunities, the privilege of being invited to be a presenter on many beautiful stages. My work as a writer is well respected and my life is pretty wonderful; but it hasn't always been that way. Out of all the major stressors one can encounter in life like; a major move, loss of a job, catastrophic illness, death of a loved one and divorce; I've experienced them all, twice, except for the divorce part. I've been married for over 40 years. I think shifts happen as you mature and grow, and that's reflected in the relationship along the way. Why am I bringing up all these stressors? Because they are the reasons why **I believe you must be at home with yourself to cope with what life throws in your path.**

Say yes, to you! Don't let fear of the unknown keep you from living the life of your dreams and going after what is right in front of you. Remember that dreams change all the time and you can make those dreams come true.

I grew up the oldest girl in a farm family. I knew I had to do my part in the family like, set the table, do the dishes, gather the eggs, feed the chickens, sweep the floor, dust the furniture and be grateful for food on the table, a roof over my head, and clothes on my back. What I didn't share with anyone was that I had dreams and I wrote in my journal about those dreams of traveling the world. I wanted to live somewhere beyond Middle America farmland. I loved reading about other cultures and life beyond my front door. I longed to fly away and be swept up in life. I was afraid these were just fantasies. Nothing that Mary, **shy, quiet Mary** would ever experience.

I decided to cautiously change my story. **I bloomed by taking a chance and stepping out of my comfort zone. I said "Yes!" to what was in front of me.** I love to sing, so I joined Mixed Chorus. When I chose to take a Speech Class, I had no idea Mr. Peterson expected all of us to also participate in the Speech Contest as part of our class. I thought I'd die of anticipation and embarrassment. Of course, I didn't die because I'm here to tell you about it. I even landed a role in the Senior Class play! By the way, now I look forward to being on stage and sharing my message that your unique story is a shimmering thread in the tapestry of the universal story, and you are the only one who can tell your story.

Little by little I learned to let go of the fear and walk in faith that I had support to follow my dreams. **My own inner strength was sustained by the fact I wasn't ever alone. I personally don't possess everything that it takes to make my dreams come true. When I do my part, God takes over to finish the job.** True, sometimes the journey has ups and downs, or the road turns in ways you would not have imagined and certainly not to land you in a situation you would have otherwise avoided had you been given a choice. Such as coping with undetermined infertility issues, or being diagnosed with breast cancer, 'twice. 'To bloom where you are planted means to live in the present moment. To SHINE at being the best you can be right now.

Sometimes you bloom in the situation you've lived in all of your life. Sometimes you are asked to stretch and grow into a new situation, and a new environment.

I not only rewrote my story to go after a dream of a college degree but I saw a way to travel and learn about one of my great loves, 'theatre.' I studied theater in London for an entire academic quarter, almost three months! I had an internship at a Fringe Theater, which was housed above a London pub. True, my college experience was the 'usual' one. I was not a fresh, faced, 18-year-old. I was a mature, 30-year-old, married woman. Family and friends were concerned I was abandoning my husband; I wasn't, I was pursuing my dream and a once in a lifetime opportunity, and I'm glad I did it.

I grew as a human being in more ways than anything that I could have read or imagined. I learned about life,

relationships and most of all, about me. In the same year, I proudly graduated from college, we joyfully became the parents of a blonde haired, blue-eyed six week old baby girl. I was now a secretary with a degree who brought those skills to my job as an Editorial Assistant on a weekly newspaper; a job I remember fondly as the best blend of being able to be a parttime employee and full time wife, and mother. I saw glimpses of a more confident me when I took a chance on going after my dreams and rewrote my story.

Do you know what? I found out that I liked her! I let her come to the surface more than just occasionally and to be honest, it scared me. I was thrilled and terrified at the same time. I was embarking on a journey to discover myself without support or encouragement from friends or family because they didn't understand the need or hunger within me. I discovered I wanted something more. I want something more for you. I've moved twice across the country because of my husband's work situation. I know what it feels like to have your world uprooted in the blink of an eye.

I don't have to imagine the shockwave that pulses through your body when the phone message states: **"All employees will not be allowed into the building and are to report to the parking lot where they would be bused to the World Theatre for a company announcement,"** or the fear that holds you hostage when you come home from picking up your ten-year-old daughter from school to find your husband at the kitchen table discussing the sale of your home with realtors.

We'd built our dream house backing up to a wooded area in a quiet cul-de-sac. We became a family in this house. Our daughter's handprints were in the cement on our back steps. She was thriving at school and I was working part-time for a weekly newspaper. We had family and friends close by. Would our new situation be as wonderful as the one we'd created and were living in now? To be honest, our lives were different every time we moved. I believe my life now is just as wonderful and full of amazing experiences as before our moves. Probably even more so because of all my blessings. I'm aware of how much abundance I have in my one, wild and precious life.

Bloom where you are planted and SHINE is all any of us can hope to do and to make a difference in this world. To make a contribution by searching for whom we are and why we are here, and deliver our gifts to those who are waiting to receive them. I've not only rewritten my story; I've spent over 30 years as a journalist supporting others to tell the story of who they are and the amazing gifts they have to share with the world. I have been a part of bringing forth both personal and professional stories into the world. It is my mission and my privilege to be an architect, mentor and cheerleader, as I assist my clients to find their voice and to share their story and to bloom, and shine!

When you honor yourself by blooming, you model for those around you so that they too, can go after their dreams and be true to themselves without compromising anyone else. Whether you have lived in the same place all your life, or you have called many addresses home; one thing has always been the same and that is, 'you.' Think about the little turtle that carries her home on her back. **Think of your inner self as your 'home,' the part of yourself that is always with you. Come home to her by getting to know who she is and what she wants.**

Be your best YOU and give whatever it is in front you your best effort. Realize that being your authentic self in the present moment is the highest compliment you can pay to the Universe. The story of you, the one that you are writing and rewriting one day at a time, one hour at a time, and one minute at a time.

Wondering how to go about rewriting your story and author of your life and consistency come home to yourself?

It's simple. I have found journaling is a valuable tool to unleash from the stories holding me back. Writing in my journal has helped me in so many ways to uncover the dreams I'd been hiding from myself and to discover ways to live my dreams.

Everything I have accomplished personally and professionally started in my journal.

I invite you commit to writing for just five minutes a day and be amazed by what will come to the surface when you take dictation from your soul.

Unleash, Come Home to yourself by creating your personal writing practice with a timed writing experience:

1. Select your writing materials. It doesn't matter whether your journal is beautiful leather bound volume or a spiral bound notebook; what I stress here is that you write in longhand and I do mean longhand. Choose a fun, fast writing pen. 'I particularly love grasping the barrel of my fountain pen and watching the purple or teal ink spill across the page.'

2. Schedule a time on your calendar where you will consistently show up and block off that time as dedicated to your writing practice.

3. Set a timer so that you focus on the writing and are not glancing at how much time has, or has not, passed.

4. Record the date and time at the top of the page, also describe your environment to help 'ground' you in the present moment. Think of this as a little ritual to let your subconscious know where you are in time and space, and a signal that your writing practice has begun.

5. You may want to add to the mood by playing some background music, or light a candle.

6. Remember to keep your hand moving. This is not the time to edit, critique, or fix your punctuation and grammar.

7. Finally, **listen and witness the deep connection between your heart and hand.**

Allow yourself the gift of at least 30-days to anchor the writing practice into your routine.

I've created a simple journal for you to download containing some of my favorite quotes for inspiration.

Just go to:

"http://yourwritingmentor.com/2016jgift/"http://yourwriti ngmentor.com/2016jgift/ and begin your writing journey today!

My Dear Bloom Reader,

I sincerely hope you take away from these words that when you unleash and come home to yourself, you will realize that you are the one you've been waiting for.

Sincerely,

Mary E. Knippel

About the Author

As a child growing up in Middle America, Mary E. Knippel dreamt of making a difference in the world. Exactly how she'd do that wasn't clear to her or anyone else since she was a shy and quiet kid who pretty much melted into the background. Today her mission is to stop you from feeling invisible. A bestselling author, inspirational speaker, and the Writer Unleashed at **YourWritingMentor.com**, she makes a difference by being your Champion, Architect and Cheerleader supporting you to unleash your story worth writing and to shine; not only in your business but in your life, as well. With a firm philosophy that ***No one can tell your story but YOU,*** Mary invites you to take pen in hand to deliver your story's unique message to the world. Using her 30 years as a journalist and the power of storytelling, she helps you gain clarity and confidence in your story and who needs to hear it.

She is fiercely committed to inspiration, compassion and synchronicity. Every heartbreak and disappointment you have ever experienced, and the way you coped with those incidents have made you who you are today; which is all part of your glorious and unique story. As a journal writer since the age of 11, Mary knows the enormous power and healing capabilities of the written word. A two-time breast cancer survivor she used writing and other creative tools in her recovery, and chronicles the results in her upcoming book, *The Secret Artist*, where she shares what she has learned to help you move from survive to thrive. Mary urges every woman, to come 'home' to herself and to be at home with herself in body, mind and spirit, and not to wait until she has a health crisis to start making herself a priority by practicing self-love and especially self-care.

Learn more about Mary's classes and workshops, request a complimentary discovery session, sign-up to receive free ongoing writing tips and techniques, or invite her to speak to your group, by visiting her website and download your free journal gift at: HYPERLINK

"http://yourwritingmentor.com" http://yourwritingmentor.com.

HYPERLINK "mailto:mary@yourwritingmentor.com" mary@yourwritingmentor.com

650-440-5616

HYPERLINK "http://yourwritingmentor.com" http://yourwritingmentor.com

HYPERLINK "http://fb.com/maryeknippel" http://fb.com/maryeknippel

HYPERLINK "http://fb.com/maryeknippel.author" http://fb.com/maryeknippel.author HYPERLINK "https://facebook.com/groups/1691124167811396" https://facebook.com/groups/1691124167811396

(Live a Life Unleashed Community with Mary E. Knippel)

HYPERLINK "http://linkedin.com/in/maryeknippel"
http://linkedin.com/in/maryeknippel

HYPERLINK "http://twitter.com/MEKnippelAuthor"
http://twitter.com/MEKnippelAuthor

HYPERLINK "http://youtube.com/user/maryeknippel"
http://youtube.com/user/maryeknippel

HYPERLINK "http://instagram.com/maryeknippelauthor"

http://instagram.com/maryeknippelauthor

HYPERLINK "http://pinterest.com/maryeknippel/"
http://pinterest.com/maryeknippel/

GROW YOUR SELF UNDER THE SUN
By Marlowe Allenbright

12:16 AM January 28, 2017 Goodbye Red Monkey. Hello Red Rooster. The turning of time on the Chinese calendar has brought in a new character to color the cycles of time through the interpretations in the Chinese Zodiac.

My second, great-granddaughter, Deanna has chosen to remain cozy in Her Mom Natalie's womb. Her choice is to crow with the sun as a rooster. Had she been born on her January 22, 2017 due date, a life of climbing as a red monkey would have been her essence according to the Chinese calendar influence. As of today, the Lunar New Year 1/28/2017 in the US, her birthdate when she arrives will include her in the tribe of Red Roosters for her lifetime. I see your choice Deanna. You shine as the morning sun and sing the praise of the morning glory. I can't wait to hear you crow.

The photo of Pallas Athena symbolizes for me how the influence from the heavens, myths and animals can color our lives. The warrior maiden seems to reflect on the owl's wisdom as she models beauty in her stance and strength though the red scarf tied to her spear. The Red Plumb on Athena's Helmet reflecting in the Sun represents the Red Fire Rooster of this Chinese New Year.

The Chinese Zodiac is comprised of twelve (12) animals that are believed to have the capacity to affect the character, development, or behavior of those born within the period when they rule. The first day of each Lunar New Year Festival will always fall sometime between January 21 and February 21, inclusive. The traditional Chinese calendar is lunisolar, like the Hebrew calendar but unlike the Western (Gregorian) solar calendar or the Islamic lunar calendar.

How important are the measures of time in our astrological calculations?

Can all systems be trusted?

Explore and judge for yourself.

I believe where seeds are scattered new growth comes forth.

For centuries, the "Farmer's Almanac" has looked to the heavens to guide the planting of crops to assure a bountiful harvest. I love the story of Johnny Appleseed. He was a man who set out to make his mark on humanity by planting seeds that apple trees might grow and flourish in his land. He eventually planted so many trees that he created groves of trees and he became known as Johnny Appleseed instead of his given name at birth. He was named John Chapman at his birth on September 26, 1774 but his mission was ordained before he was born. His tombstone bears the inscription:

HE LIVED FOR OTHERS:

That was his destiny. I believe he was driven by innate forces of stars and sun and moon, just as all human beings are, determined by the day they are born. I am destined to be a writer yet caught in the indecision of creativity I am forced to choose a favorite child if I would succeed in the craft, and so my inner dialogue begins; but I value them all! How can I choose? How can I choose between all my offspring of ideas and settle on one as my first, my only for this writing?

(Self-doubt and indecision my nemesis in commitment gains inspiration from W.H. Murray.)

"Until one is committed, there is hesitancy, the chance to draw back, always ineffectiveness… Whatever you can do or dream you can, begin it. Boldness has genius, power and magic in it!"

And then another voice says, YES! Let's keep that escape route open, that hatch that would allow me to escape into the vastness and be lost in space. Yet Fate has lead me and pulled me back on track from all my efforts to stray away from my destiny. How scary is that still? Oh, ego I may say as I agree with all my inner critics. Who do you think you are? What makes you think you are so special? You can do anything you want. So why aren't you doing it? It's like the flowers confronting Alice in Wonderland or the proverbial question from the caterpillar, "Who are you?"

I love both Disney images. The flowers are beautiful in their nature but quite boring in their singing their egoist praises in "A Lovely Sunday Afternoon." The caterpillar is in an elevated or drugged state of mind asking Alice, "Who are you". But as we all know the butterfly is soon to evolve from that intellectual larva. And flowers come and go ever evolving their perfection. "Imagine that! Being bullied by flowers and caterpillars about my identity?" No way! I say. "I am that which I am!" "But, ok I don't know for sure, who am I really?"

Perhaps, dear reader, you've also experienced inner dialogues and the voices in your head? Have you ever struggled with inner critics and conflicting thoughts, ideas? I want to encourage you to remember to be kind and patient with yourself. It's very difficult to stuff an immortal being into a single identity for the span of a lifetime. That's why theater is such a favorite past time.

It reminds our inner being that we are not alien projections of our stories on the screen of Life. Our lives have meaning! We matter! We are all destined to bloom. Although the seed may wander far from home, the acorn always grows to be the oak.

Your DNA seeds the maturation of your existence to grow, mature, and bear fruit to regenerate through your legacy. What is your legacy? How will you issue your stamp on humanity?

Do you play card games? What's your favorite? When I was eight years old, on New Year's Eve, I became an aunt to my Nephew Richard. My sister-in-law Joan introduced me to broadcast pinochle. I loved playing Pinochle. This game intrigued me with its four cards hidden from view until a player took the bid. Problem was the game required four players. Most of the time there was just Joan and me and with just two players it held no mystery. So, because I am as smart as I am, an idea came to me to suit (pun intended) my longing. As I love and appreciate the mystery.

The mystery always drew me to want to possess those mystery cards for better or worse. So, I created a modified set of game rules that allowed the four mystery cards in the deal for two players and increased my delight in the game. **I want to encourage you to make choices to change the rules and play life according to how you are made and what delights you?**

Since that creative triumph at the age of 8, I'm fascinated by what I've learned from the deck of fifty-two playing cards. In fact, I developed a system to gain insights about ourselves from a deck of 52 playing cards. Every birthday is represented by one of the cards and anyone born on December 31st like my nephew Richard is card 53 "The Joker." John Chapman was a Jack of Hearts; card 11 "Universal Love Card." Just as a packet of seeds holds the potential for the growth of a flower, a playing card holds the essence of destiny for each human being's natal day. So, it is with the magic hidden in the message of each of the 52 playing cards and the joker. It is a blueprint for growth to assure the experiences of the incarnating child can yield its destiny. It provides guidance for playing with a full deck.

Your card is your compass to live the life of your dreams. The best part is there is a mathematical basis these "Cards of Illumination" hold. There are many parallels to nature in this tarot calendar. There are four seasons and four suits. There are red and black cards and day and night. There are 13 cards in each suit and 13 moons in a year. There are 52 weeks in a year and 52 cards in the deck. Once we know our card we can use it to create a wonderful life by following the life guidance in our "Dream Deck" represented by the periodic table of the cards. I was born on May 6th so I am a King of Diamonds; card number 39 "Authority in Values."

Starting high school, I was an eager beaver to take a full schedule of classes in my freshman year. As a sophomore, studying chemistry, I was required to learn the periodic table of the elements. It was boring and meaningless to me. Then I had an epiphany through the order it contained and the combination of the elements to create new substances. I was intrigued by the precision that when two hydrogen atoms (H_2) combined with one oxygen atom (O) a new element was formed. It was water (H_2O) the essence of life on earth. I loved the mathematical certainty that represented the creative potential in knowing the combinations.

A realization came to me that I was not meant to be learning this table by rote. Can you relate to that inner urge that arises from somewhere almost unknown and yet so familiar? For me it was a response to the creative urge. Forces arose from within me as I began the expansion of my family constellation. In June 1960, I graduated from high school in 3 years instead of four. Dan Viola and Margo Reuter married on October 29th the following year. A week less than a year later, we gave birth to Donna Lynn and Deborah Jean was born two weeks and a day less than a year later.

Destiny pulled me to keep my timeline with the universe. Now that I know my Sun Card I have a track to follow based on mathematical certainty through the periodic table of my almanac. It guides me to be bold and fulfill the potential from my starry seed and relate with compassion to all Nature.

My goal is to speak to you through words that you may glean some seeds of wisdom from the fruit of my labors to nurture your garden. Can you believe we reach our full potential in life, not by straining to over achieve which only leads to stress and burnout, but by blossoming naturally into the fullness of who we are?

Then visit us at www.healthisland.us to find your "Sun Card" and Grow Your Self.

Under the Sun
Every challenge we encounter,
Comes to us from a higher power.
All the lessons we must learn,
Are monitored with a deep concern.
And Love comes forth in every action,
Though we may not see with satisfaction.
For our myopic little eye,
Tries hard to stick with only try.
While in the greater scheme of things,
Each One is meant for wondrous deeds.
Expos to show our fellow man,
The glories of earth from which I Am.
And in the end to set with glory,
The magnificence of Each One's Story.
Marlowe Allenbright 1-21-2017

Here's my oldest great-granddaughter, Taleena she's a Nine of Diamonds, card 35 "The Giver." With the sun on her right shoulder, she's beckoning you to take a step forward toward your destiny to bloom and SHINE!

About the Author

Growing up in the time before television, "Margo" used to listen to her favorite radio program *The Shadow*, as she did her homework. Her mother marveled that she could do two things at once. "Margo" was a member of the National Honor Society when she graduated from High School in 1960, married her high school sweetheart the following year, began her vocation of motherhood with two daughters, and then divorced. A few years later she married a widower father of three, moved to Massachusetts, and then to California in 1978. There "Margo" obtained her Life and Health Insurance license, began her chameleon career in the financial services industry and became a Certified Financial Planner. Her desire; is to help her clients gain peace of mind. She guided them to understanding the basics for protecting themselves against potential risks and determining their goals for the future. In 1987 "Margo" reinvented herself and changed the name on her birth certificate and blossomed as

Marlowe Allenbright, free from the baggage associated with her earlier incarnations. Today she's still doing two things at once; she maintains her successful career in the health insurance industry, guiding those who "come of age" to choose their best path for Medicare choices. At the same time, she is educating them to explore alternative systems for self-care that fit their life blueprint. Marlowe encourages, "Follow your life path, fulfill your heart's desire, and leave a legacy of love."

Enjoy a free vitality planner at
www.iseekwellness.net
1-877-752- 9475 or 1-707-431-1003
mallenbright@yahoo.com
www.facebook.com/marlowe.allenbright,
www.linkedin.com/in/marlowe-allenbright-43645a5
www.marloweallenbright.com
www.healthisland.us
 www.medicaremaven.info
www.iseekwellness.net

Section 4
BLOOM

Discover how to build and grow your gifts to full bloom.... not someday but today. Discover tips, tools and insights to help you grow the beautiful gift of who you are to share with the world.

FORGIVENESS CAN BRING OUT YOUR SHINE!
By Carolyn CJ Jones

At the age of fifty-two, I had my first taste of peace from childhood experiences. Along with it came freedom that rocked my world! Until that point, I had lived my life an angry, bitter, blaming victim. I knew no other way. Even though I wore a smile, I was miserable inside and I'm sure it was difficult for others to be around me. Yet, in an instant, that all changed the day I stumbled upon forgiveness. What I learned in the process of coming to forgive is vast. It's hard for me to go through all the experiences.

I've had in the period of time from when I was fifty-two to my current sixty-four years and remain blind to the wisdom and blessings that I've gained. It's easy, as a person graced with consciousness and awareness, to see the world with awe and wonder, with great gratitude. It is this, the wonder, the blessings, that I want you to know, see, and experience, for these are the basis of your shine! Peace and freedom can become yours, as they have become mine. I hope this chapter prompts you to begin the journey of awareness, while applying the truths that are contained herein.

My passion is to hear that you are experiencing changes that are leading to freedom and all it includes. If you're now struggling with an issue, resentment, or story, know that within each of the truths presented in this chapter lies a golden nugget of hard-won wisdom that you can use right now to begin the journey to the life you desire. From this chapter, you learn to bloom wherever you are in any moment and shine your light upon the world.

Let's start with mindset. I could lament all day about what I missed in my first fifty-two years. Instead, I choose to be tremendously happy for any person, especially if they're young (under forty), who has successfully changed their life from one of resentment, bitterness, and misery, to one of happiness, peace, and grace. I am thrilled to know their journey will be filled with great richness for the bulk of their adulthood.

Truth # 1: You can choose your mindset.

You can be disparaging and discouraging, see the glass as half empty, or, you can see it as half-full and choose a more uplifting attitude. It's up to you. The more you're able to maintain an uplifted mindset, the greater is your ability to bloom and shine.

Truth # 2: Be of service.

The fact is we have each experienced things in our lives that did not go the way we'd hoped and planned. Rather than be upset about it, we can turn around our feelings of sadness by recognizing and offering encouragement and support to others who are attempting to create better lives. Being of service to another in this way is a very rich and empowering experience.

Truth # 3: Be willing to change.

The ability to change is not dependent upon age. Instead, it depends upon your willingness. The more willing you are to try new things, expand, and grow, the more you can flow into change. The more willing you become, the more you can reach the inner 'you,' and learn to express that deep, all-knowing voice. That voice has control over whether or not you bloom and shine. Willingness is the key.

Before going on to truth four, I'd like to say more about my passion for leading people to peace and freedom. To understand why I'm so passionate, I share here about my life until forgiveness came along, how forgiveness happened, and what life holds for me now. This requires me to refer to my childhood, which I am hesitant to do for fear of hurting family. Suffice it to say, my experiences left me very confused, hurt, and terrified.

I went to college to become a nurse. While there, my suppressed feelings of shame, worthlessness, and depression began to surface. These feelings stemmed from what I experienced as a child. My poor confidence and self-esteem became an issue with which I struggled for many years and still do some days. I didn't know how to cope when my feelings came up. All I knew to do was to close myself off while acting as if I was happy, even though I was dying inside. Senior year of college, I discovered how very nicely alcohol numbed my feelings. Armed with that knowledge, I discovered a year later that drugs enhanced that escape, and I proceeded to drink and drug for the next thirty years.

The landing was excruciating and I share it with you here because it contains wonderful truths. At twenty-eight, I met and married a fellow alcoholic, who was very stunted in his emotional growth, as was I. We had some great and fun times, yet as a whole, the marriage was volatile and filled with verbal and emotional abuse that went both ways. We were both highly functioning, held high-level jobs of responsibility and performed extremely well, so neither of us could get serious about other's concerns of our drinking problem. We rejected all offers of help. "We don't need it!" we snapped defiantly.

Truth # 4: Substance use and abuse knows no boundaries and has nothing to do with willpower, intelligence, or level of performance in life.

I fooled myself into thinking that because I was a highly functioning adult, with high-functioning jobs, I couldn't be an alcoholic. "Clearly," I thought, "I do not have a problem if I can hold these jobs down and get these great performance reviews!" I was wrong about that and could have stopped the unceasing drama that governed the insanity of my life, many years before I actually did. **When you are free of dependence upon substances, you enhance your ability to shine at a deep level.**

After seventeen years of marriage, my husband and I moved from Colorado where we'd met and lived together, to

Sausalito, California to live aboard a forty-five-foot sailboat. Our dream was to fix her up, sail the Bay, and then go cruising around the world. Three years into it, the threats that I'd leave the marriage finally played out when I met and fell deeply in love with a dock mate. Thinking we were soul mates and that he felt as I did, I left my marriage to make myself available to him. Come to find out, the dock mate didn't care for me. I was devastated, emotionally shattered, and for two months could only drink and cry. I hit rock bottom.

Finally, out of desperation, I sought sobriety on March 6, 2001. Raw and reeling from the rejection of my supposed soul mate, and terrified to be alone on my own after a twenty-year marriage, I proceeded to go to four or five 12-Step meetings a day for a year-and-a-half. I was *so* emotionally raw, and it was *so* difficult for me, this action was what it took to keep from drinking, and to keep me from slipping away in my grief over the unrequited love.

Truth # 5: It is difficult to leave a relationship knowing you will be alone, even when there is verbal, emotional, physical, or sexual abuse.

In hindsight, I see how terribly unjust and unfair staying in the marriage was to my husband and to me. At the very least, it was hurtful and disrespectful to each of us. I now understand that leaving might have been difficult for me, as well as terrifying, yet, it was the honest and most humane action to take. When you can be honest and act from a place of integrity, you really blossom and shine. And, **you can grow into cherishing your time alone, so you are not lonely.**

Truth # 6: It is possible to have a wonderful life without drugs and alcohol!

My life has become *amazing* in sobriety! Yours can become so too, if you think you have a problem. There are so many warmhearted souls who have been where you may be now. You can ask them for help and they'll be there for you, with you.

I discovered forgiveness four years into sobriety and my life changed forever. I realized that I forgave my past after a year of feeling compassion for my parents' wounds. You see, at three years sober, I realized I'd done to the men in my life the same extremely hurtful and damaging thing my father had done to me. I repeatedly called them worthless and said they'd never amount to anything. This was *horrible,* and the thing is, what I'd said didn't even apply to them; I meant it about *myself.* This was a *huge* epiphany! It stood to reason that *all those years* my father called me worthless and said I would never amount to anything, he meant it about himself and not about me! Suddenly, I saw him as a fellow human being who was wounded, just like me. I felt compassion for his wounds, and for my mother's, too. After a year of jumping back and forth between anger and compassion, I realized one day that forgiveness had gently found me; the peace and freedom I felt were immediate and immense.

Truth # 7: Hurt people, hurt.

In other words, when a person is hurting, they often lash out at others in the way they were hurt themselves. It is possible to look with the heart of compassion and to see their hurt as being wounded. When you can do this, you are on your way to forgiveness. You begin to really bloom into your fullness as a being at the point you become compassionate toward others *and* toward yourself. Since my discovery of forgiveness, I have grown my ability for practicing willingness, surrender or letting go, and gratitude.

I have grown a deep, deep appreciation of self and others. In my work, I gently lead women into their story, as together we weave another way to see, from a different perspective. It is incredibly empowering to look deeply at your actions, behaviors, and thoughts by conducting fact-finding self-appraisals on an ongoing basis. As you soul-search, you become able to choose what you'd like to grow in yourself and what you'd rather extinguish.

Truth # 8: You have a choice in every matter in your life.

You may not like one of the two options, yet, that choice still exists. You simply choose not to take it. When you begin to say, "I choose to do "xyz" instead of abc," instead of saying, "I can't," or, "I won't," you feel more empowered.

Forgiveness is the choice you make to hurt and suffer less, even though you're wounded. This is the ultimate choice you can make to assure that you bloom right where you're planted and shine your brightest light. Once forgiveness came to me in 2005, things began to change. Yet, it's been within the past year that I have really deepened my own ability to blossom, to bloom, and to shine my light brightly, proudly, with feelings of great worth and goodness. I am so grateful!

Truth # 9: The practice of gratitude will *transform* your life!

It is difficult to see anything good in a situation when your life is crumbling around you. Still, even in darkness, you can choose to look for something you appreciate about the experience. If, in the midst of turmoil, you can find one thing for which you are grateful, you set yourself free from the hold the turmoil has on you.

For example, the unrequited love debacle was just that – a debacle. It took me seven years after it happened to realize that if this experience had not occurred, I'd still be in my abusive marriage, still drinking (if I was even alive) and still angry at my parents and the world. Today, I am grateful for that excruciating time in my life because, 1. It pried me out of a horribly dysfunctional marriage, 2. It got me sober, 3. It led me to find forgiveness for my parents, and 4. It got me started guiding others to freedom when the light of forgiveness dawned for them. Do I want to repeat it? No way. Gratitude can still occur even though I never want to do it again. When you see your own 'debacle' in an appreciative light, then your life changes. The change occurs because you are willing to make a choice to look at things from a new perspective. Bravo! Please note that it takes willingness first and once you're willing, you can willingly choose gratitude. When you see with eyes and heart that appreciate everything around and within you, then life becomes more beautiful, more pleasing.

Truth # 10: Forgiveness can find you.

Forgiveness finds you when you have created a space in your heart that is open and filled with compassion and gratitude. When you become willing to let go of your own hurt and pain, blame and anger, and fill your soul with compassion for another's pain as well as gratitude for the experience, you become ready to receive forgiveness and all the wonderful benefits that are far beyond your wildest imagination!

The first step to living this life is to identify whether you have a story that is running it. Maybe it's the divorce, settlement, the kids, your childhood, or the neighbor. Whatever it is, this is your story and when you change that story, you change your life. I invite you to get my gift to you, a report from my heart to yours, *The Beginning: Change Your Story, Change Your Life*. You learn the signs that you might have a story and what to do about it. It's available at www.carolyncjjones.com. I hope you have discovered these truths to be useful. May they join you in your journey as you bloom, blossom profusely, and shine!

About the Author

Carolyn CJ Jones is a forgiveness guide and coach, speaker, multi-award-winning author, and creator of the *Change Your Story, Change Your Life* programs. She also created *Freedom from Resentment: The Art of Forgiveness* that she teaches in drug/alcohol treatment centers. She taught this course in San Quentin Prison to men nearing parole. Having spent thirty adult years as an angry, bitter, blaming, victim over her upbringing, drinking and drugging the entire time, CJ knows well the life of resentment, the life of the empty glass. Finally, beaten to an all-time emotional low, she sought sobriety.

Four years later, she stumbled across forgiveness for her past. The peace and freedom were immediate. Today, she sees life as a refillable glass, positive, and filled with wonder. She bloomed where she was planted so she could shine her light brightly; she now guides others to do this. As a registered nurse for twenty-seven years, CJ demonstrated her abilities to design and manage a ground breaking program while employed by the Colorado State Medicaid Department. She created, developed, and managed the program that allowed medically fragile children to be cared for at home instead of living in the hospital's intensive care unit.

Additionally, her training abilities were demonstrated when she developed and produced over eighty Statewide trainings for hundreds of health care professionals providing care in the program. Writing has always been a joy for CJ. She formally utilized her skills while working with Colorado Medicaid, as she was responsible to write the annual report to the Legislature.

She also wrote the regulations, Policy and Procedure Manual, and the application packet for the program she developed. When that job ended, her writing went to the back burner. CJ's soul's desire to write came into being again with the writing, production, and self-publication of her award-winning book, *Opening the Gates of the Heart: A Journey of Healing*.

In her spare time, she loves being with Izzy, her kitty. She also enjoys tending her plants, decorating, and writing material for her programs and for submission to magazines. CJ lives in the San Francisco Bay Area. 1-415-883-8325

Connect with her:

cj@carolyncjjones.com
http://carolyncjjones.com
http://facebook.com/carolyncjjones
http://facebook.com/carolyncjjonesspeaker
http://linkedin.com/in/carolyncjjones
@carolyncjjones

CHOOSING TO LOVE AGAIN
By Jim T. Chong

"Let YOUR GROWTH inspire others and Let YOUR SHINE illuminate their path during the times of darkness. Will adversity be your FINISH LINE, or your STARTING LINE for something great?"

~Jim T. Chong

When you see, sunlight radiate as it starts to illuminate the sky in the early morning, the rays give life and joy to another day. This is the "SHINE" that helps life flourish and bloom. As we bloom, we are also able to "SHINE" for others to help them grow. I realize that light shines the brightest in the darkest of places. Through life, we can take the darkest moments in our lives and use them to help us to shine even brighter illuminating a path for others.

"Life And All Its Splendor..."

Reflecting back and as I listen to one of the greatest groups of all time sing their song, "September", I feel so inspired and filled with gratitude. The song by the nostalgic group Earth, Wind, & Fire would start with the rhythmically unique tempo and beat as the horns play in the song and the lead singer would start to sing the words with the reflective thought, "Do you remember, the 21st night in September…".

This was an incredible song that was to signal the beginning of a new life for me as I proudly walked down the aisle and out of the church with my ever so beautiful bride. I had actually facilitated and coordinated the music for literally hundreds of weddings before…but this one was special…this one was my very own! This was one of the best moments of my life! From that moment, I had been able to have so many wonderful experiences and adventures in life. If you have experienced true love and marry the person of your dreams you know exactly what I am talking about. Who can ever forget their honeymoon and the wonderfully passionate nights that would be followed by having our own family and great friends? Life was good!

"Life Happens!"

Fast forward to today where I am faced with the memories and reflections of those prior years which are so clear and vivid but at the same time so blurred. Having experienced so many blessings through marriage, being surrounded by numerous friends and of course overcoming and learning from various family and personal challenges for many years. I thought I could withstand almost anything. Boy, was I wrong! **It wasn't until I was confronted with the stark reality that my own life's course would be altered for the worse as issues would arise that we could not overcome.** With a failing marriage and only a whisper of a relationship with God remaining, I needed to desperately come up with a solution. Well, I knew that my then faithful wife's attitude and demeanor would eventually turn around…" She is always able to boomerang back around, right???". Not this time. I never really lost hope until I lost my wife. If you have experienced a significant separation through death or divorce you understand the feelings and pain of loss.

Since then, I have reflected many times on what I had done wrong. Why was our marriage unable to survive the challenges we faced? I never had a "Plan B" for marriage as it was never an option to have my own marriage fail. Thus, I was completely unprepared, caught off guard and broadsided. Through many painful nights I sat in reflection going through arguably the toughest, most relentless, and painful experience I had ever known. The pain was an emotional pain of separation and in this case a loss of something that I held so dear not just from virtue but even from deeper within myself. Not only would it be a separation with my spouse but a split of my family unit as a whole.

My way of dealing with things is not to isolate myself, but rather the opposite. Already an individual that always sought to serve others, this extremely devastating situation propelled me even further to help further "support the greater good.", but it would now be alone. For the most part, I haven't spent too much time looking back...but that was only after taking many good hard looks at my life, "What I could have done differently?" I asked myself and of course reflecting on the moment I accepted the reality of the situation asking myself also occasionally, "What just happened?"

After many sleepless nights of contemplation and trying to reach resolution with myself, I have decided that this event in life was in some odd way to prepare me for something bigger and also help me truly not just understand but empathize with those that go through what we call "LIFE". **This situation combined with helping serve my father, whose memory is failing at the time of this writing, has taught me so many valuable lessons.** However, to reach these lessons, I needed to truly make some solid decisions and come to some very important conclusions for myself. I had always been one that has been able to help others "overcome" but now it was time to personally put into practice the advice and help that I had given to so many others.

Dealing with the pain of separation is one of the most difficult things one can go through. My friend described separation by divorce as synonymous with "having someone die on you, only you get to see them over and over again and year after year...especially when kids are involved." I have always heard that when you become "single again", your primary friends change from married couples to people that have gone through the same thing. Wow! I can't explain it, but having had my primary close friendships with married couples. I find that today, much of my immediate demographics have indeed changed. Coping with the reality of the situation, it honestly was a very easy decision for me to truly decide to give wholeheartedly to others and help them reach their dreams. **One thing I did realize though after a few years...that as my love for others increased my love for myself decreased which was not at all good or healthy.** It no longer was at all about me, but entirely about others. I am sharing authentically and transparently, as I took this to an extreme and I literally removed myself from the equation.

From this revelation, I was able to course correct (which is by no means an easy task). I had to rebuild my thinking starting with where I would fit into the equation and start to love myself again. Being a professional Master Emcee and Radio Show Personality for a major network program, I am so blessed to be a part of literally so many causes and communities. I am always still learning to make sure I actively love and value myself in everything I do. I truly understand more than ever that every moment we have is a blessing. And that every breath we take while still on earth is a breath that no one else will have an opportunity to take. **I do believe I have a fiduciary responsibility to never take for granted even a single breath.**

From my experience and discussion with some experts dealing with grief and overcoming some emotional trauma of some major life situation, I realized that there are some key factors to help you work through those times. I found these extremely helpful and a major component in being able to shine during adversity.

KEYS TO RELEASING YOUR ABILITY TO SHINE

Decide to love and forgive yourself and accept that life happens.

This was a very important part of my starting to be able to feel good again. During these times, I started to look at situations and asked myself if I intentionally did anything wrong from my perspective. For me, I needed to verbalize the situation and actually say out loud many times "I did the best I could at the time." It was a while until I accepted the situation, then had to deal with my own acceptance of myself and that **I DESERVED TO BE LOVED**. And eventually got to the point where I did forgive myself. This was not a single event, but a process to get to that point. Remember, **YOU DESERVE TO BE LOVED!**

Understand that the healing is a process and not a single event.

The irony of this point is that I am an active part of "Healings In Motion", a 10+ year non-profit dedicated to stroke awareness and brain health as well as caregiving. In the events, I get to participate and facilitate for this organization. We talk a considerable amount about healing. I didn't realize the emotional trauma people endured whether it be a loss of a loved one through death or serving as a caregiver. Now being a part time caregiver for my father and having gone through the separation with my ex-spouse, I am understanding how the wounds do not just instantaneously get better, but rather it is a continual process of healing. Knowing what to expect is one of the best things that have helped me be able to anticipate how things will be. I can then set up realistic expectations to heal. Healing is a journey and a process. Be kind and supportive to yourself on this journey.

Surround yourself with some good friends that know will be there for you and lift you up.

I am fortunate enough to be surrounded by people who are genuinely about helping others either through an organization they have formed or take an active part in helping others on a continual basis either formally as a professional or as an involved volunteer. Many of these people have also experienced major life events that have made them stronger. They are people that I can always go to that truly know me and will listen, but also tell me the things I need to hear. They inspire me to keep going and I realize that I can do the same for others. Join, create, or look for a supportive community to walk with and beside you on the healing journey.

Take an active role in helping others.

It is no hidden secret that when you give to others, there is a sense of personal accomplishment and sometimes even a euphoria knowing that you have done something significant for others. When you get involved, you understand that you are not alone and it also helps you become more grateful when you encounter people that have gone through and endured even more than you may have. I found that through different people's circumstances and situations, I was able to learn so much about life through their victories and adversities. Hearing the stories helped me understand more about myself and in many ways, have enriched my life. Knowing that I have made a difference for others helps remind me that **MY LIFE MATTERS**. Reach out and help others. Remember, **YOUR LIFE MATTERS**.

Decide To Be Grateful

Take time to reflect on the many blessings around you.

"The Best Teacher"

My life experience is by no means unique. I share my story in hopes that it inspires those that can relate to not give up. We can give up in so many ways when we are called to move forward. Life is truly a journey with unexpected events. Chose not to give up, but choose to find the value in every situation and card life deals you. During the times in your life when things are going well, never forget those difficult times and let them propel you to help others. During the times, you face adversity, seek understanding and the value of your life's experience. Never give up and become stagnant. Keep moving forward not just for yourself, but also for others that may be watching. Let the experience of life allow you to grow and "Bloom where you are planted and SHINE!". Make the decisions that support you and enrich your life so that you may be an even greater blessing to others. ***The choice is always yours...to decide whether or not to LOVE AGAIN! But it begins with you learning how to love yourself.***

One of the best things I have done to heal is to write. I had composed a song that was used as the 2014 theme for a 10+ year non-profit organization "Healings In Motion" that is dedicated to Stroke Awareness, Care Giving, and Healing as a whole. It has been instrumental on my journey in life and continually helps me and others to reflect and think about how I can help others in their healing process...by simply being there for them and taking and initiating an active role.

Enjoy...and here is to your healing and journey.

AGENTS FOR PROGRESS

by Jim T. Chong

When I look at all the people I have seen this past year, some were touched with happiness while others filled with fear.

Some just need a warm embrace while others need a prayer. When they look deep into your eyes will they see someone who cares.

Are you an Agent For Progress...more than just a notion? Are you an Agent For Progress

joining...Healings In Motion today!

You may be a husband or you may be a wife.
You know it's a simple choice to save somebody's life.
If you've ever seen someone in deep and dark despair...you know it's an easy choice to reach out and to care.
You can be an Agent For Progress...
more than just a notion.
Be an Agent For Progress joining...
Healings In Motion today!

You may be a beacon of hope or a whisper in the night...for someone who feels all alone but still chooses to fight.
You take an honest look you're busy this is true. But someday this beacon of hope may be waiting there for you.
We are an Agent For Progress...more than just a notion.
We are an Agent For Progress joining...Healings In Motion today!

About the Author

Jim T. Chong is a Master Emcee, Publicist, licensed financial professional, and the founder of Solutions4Life, the Wok Star, and a radio personality in the Greater Sacramento area on MONEY 1055FM as the Wok Star on "Rush Hour For

Success". Jim helps people develop their story, speaking, and presence. He serves on the Executive Team of several established non-profit and cause-based communities and organizations in his local area. He excels in helping support those that wish to gain more influence and exposure in their local community by helping support them and "SHINE" either as their Master Emcee or through social media.

Jim supports and facilitates several workshops and programs such as the "Central Valley Recovery Awareness Preventing Strokes" (CV-RAPS) monthly program which is at St. Joseph's Medical Center in San Joaquin County on behalf of Healings In Motion (http://www.healingsinmotion.org) and also provides bi-monthly inspiration, personal development, and character/leadership talks for the Central Valley Asian American Chamber Of Commerce IMC program and other organizations.

Jim is a sought-after emcee who consistently speaks in front of hundreds of people monthly. He has also emceed the Vietnamese Lunar Flower Festival in the city of Sacramento as well as the Chinese New Year's Parade and Festival in Stockton City where thousands with thousands in attendance. Jim is a sought-after Master Emcee who has served as the Master Of Ceremonies to various established organizations and speaker venues including the Annual Asian Festival in the town of Locke, California which is the last remaining self-contained Chinese town in the United States.

In May 2016, Jim had recently briefly appeared on the national program for the Travel Channel in Ghost Adventures. Jim has also helped produce award winning short films and is a co-owner of In Motion Theatre

Company along with Cami Ferry which gives a portion of its profits back to a designated cause.

Through the "Wok Star" personality, Jim is passionate about advancing culture, community, and commerce by establishing collaborative venues and is looking forward to the launch of his global network show "Live Strong America-News To Inspire" and is currently launching "The CEO Leadership Corner" with Jon Taber.

He is also helping people tell their story through his publishing company Wok Star Multimedia Publishing.

He gets his fulfillment supporting the greater good by helping individuals' dreams come true by developing strategies for their money, message, and branding.

Connect with Jim:

jtc.wokstar@gmail.com

Phone Number 209.534.8000

Websites

http://www.TheWokStar.com
http://www.thewokstar.com/

http://www.RushHourForSuccess.com
http://www.rushhourforsuccess.com/

Facebook page(s)

http://www.facebook.com/RushHourForSuccess
http://www.facebook.com/RushHourForSuccess
http://www.facebook.com/WokStarProduction
http://www. facebook.com/WokStarProduction
Twitter handle TheWokStar

MY BLOSSOMING JOURNEY
By Catherine M Laub

I am excited to share my journey and success as a blossoming flower. I began as a mother and grandmother but blossomed into an author, speaker, radio show host, psychic, medium, spiritual guide and consultant. This was all a surprise to me because I thought my life was always going to revolve around my poor health. These health challenges overpowered my life, but God and my Angels had different plans for me. I am 59 and married to a wonderful man, Tony. We have 7 children, 15 grandchildren, and 1 great-grandchild. I worked for Tony for 13 years. He bought the company I was working for, partially because of my ongoing health problems.

He gave me flexibility and I worked from home most of the time. He closed the company in 2013 due to the effects of the great recession. It left me stressed because my poor health prevented me from working a full-time job. Because of my significant health issues, I now receive Disability Benefits but plan to be self-sufficient at some point in my blossoming journey.

I learned through my spirituality and self-help guides how to think positively and use affirmations to put me on a path of healing. Before my confidence became resilient, I didn't leave my house, not even to go shopping. My trips were only to doctor's offices and Tony did all the shopping, and even house cleaning. Because I am a worthy woman Tony helps me in most situations daily. He supports me in my business ventures and helps me at craft fairs and events.

My health got worse because with most of my colon removed in 2012, I was "living" in the bathroom.

I spent a lot of time watching television between my bathroom 'visits'. My quality of life was missing. My physical health affected my mental illness, and vice versa. I downloaded self-help programs and lessons on spirituality. This information didn't settle in my consciousness until August, 2014, when I impulsively attempted suicide. During an argument with Tony I reacted by grabbing my pills. Once I was in the hospital I knew things would get better. This wasn't my first hospitalization, but my only attempt. So, I knew the process of getting better.

God and my Angels answered my prayer. I asked for help to stop taking some of the 22 medications I was on and start feeling better. I had to get to this point to put things into perspective. While hospitalized the team of doctors cut out many of my medications. **I recognized my assignment is to help others more in a greater way. The difference this time was realizing something we all know but never put into action. We should always put ourselves first! Put the oxygen mask on first, and then help those around you.** Once out of the hospital that is what I did. I focused on myself both physically and mentally with a new community of doctors. I spent more time learning how to grow my business and expanding my reach to others.

My angels gave me a mission to speak out about mental illness to let people know **'It is OK'**. My campaign is "Brighten Your Day with Turquoise", where I share my own experiences and welcome-others to open up about theirs. I am not embarrassed to say I have a mental illness. I recognize that I had to experience certain things to go forward sharing with others for guidance. Even though I continue to have many health issues, I chose to go forward with my business, and I want you to know it can be done. I now help people gain the knowledge they are seeking to begin or continue on their spiritual and/or healing journey. One of my messages is have faith and know you can always pull through anything!!! Another message is you are not alone. Since September 2015 I have contributed to 8 anthologies and continue to write for others. My stories have all centered on my healing journey and spirituality. Here I share more about my business journey and how I accomplished so much in just a few years.

My biggest recommendation is to always be authentic! By doing so you attract positive people and positive situations. In conversation, I don't hold back in fear of embarrassment. The more authentic I am the more respected and liked I am.

I used to call myself an Angel Communicator and Card Reader but have progressed and now am a psychic and medium as well. I stumbled on this journey with a life coach in 2010. Donna did angel readings every session and I inquired how I could learn this. I instantly signed up for lessons, and most of the readings came easy for me. Almost instantly I heard my angels tell me I would make a living doing readings.

Once I was working publicly at psychic fairs my skills advanced quickly. I love sharing messages with everyone. It makes them happy to know their family and friends are around, and it gives me a great feeling to know I helped them. I have compassion and relate to others situations due to my experience with negative health and life situations. Being an empath brings feelings into my readings. (Empath: feeling that you understand and share another person's emotions)

My programs help others experience the satisfaction and excitement I feel. I teach Vision Board and Creation Journaling, Angel Communication, and have a spiritual meetup where we discuss many areas of spirituality and self-help. I created online courses to be downloaded and studied at one's own pace. I highly suggest joining organizations to network with others and learn how to advance in business. Two top organizations I am involved with are the Women's Prosperity Network and the Independent Business Women's Circle. A great deal can be learned from these groups and the women are very supportive of each other.

I began to take new steps to attract customers, and shared my story in other collaborative books. It was slow moving at first, and then once it merged together I knew the direction to promote my message. I do readings at craft fairs and other events. I created and continually update my own website. I also designed my business cards and create special flyers for my events. I created a free gift and joined Joint Venture Giveaways on line to promote my business and am a member of many Facebook groups and interact frequently.

"The meaning of the color turquoise is open communication and clarity of thought. It helps to open the lines of communication between the heart and the spoken word. It presents as a friendly and happy color enjoying life. In color psychology, turquoise controls and heals the emotions creating emotional balance and stability." "The soul always knows what to do to heal itself. The challenge is to silence the mind." - Caroline Myss. Everyone should know how very important it is to share when you are experiencing depression, anxiety, OCD (Obsessive Compulsive Disorder), Seasonal Affective Disorder, Bipolar or any other symptom of mental illness. By doing so, you can get on the right path and feel better. The stigma is not what it was in the past.

You can learn about the options available to you at NAMI

(National Alliance of Mental Illness) http://www.nami.org/

Call the NAMI helpline 800-950-NAMI or email info@nami.org In addition to NAMI State Organizations, there are more than 950 NAMI Affiliates in communities across the country.

Although I talk about getting through a stressful situation, I still allow it to affect me at times because I don't always follow my own advice.

There are many layers to go through to achieve my goals; and what God wants for me, WHEN God wants it. My light is shining from the inside and blossoming out. God is good and keeps sending my healing angels to take care of one situation at a time. We can overcome health issues when we put our minds to it. I realize the road is rocky but it has to be to gain experience.

With my combined skills, I help others achieve their potential without all the obstacles that get in the way. I plant the seeds and suggest new beginnings for growth.

My confidence grew rapidly this past year and I am now a Radio Show Host of Spiritual Destinations. I interview people about their own spirituality and success in life. These shows are broadcast in many areas and can be listened to as recordings.

Eventually I will open a store/retreat center where I will sell spiritual, self-help, religious and inspirational items. I will have a living room setting for people to come relax while having a stressful day. This center will combine spirituality and mental health so anyone needing guidance will be welcome.

I wrote the following on Facebook in 2015: *"BUT MY MESSAGE IS: I AM STILL GOING!! Part of this message is if you have setbacks, plan on attending events, etc., and psyche yourself up because that will be the distraction you need to make it happen. I didn't leave my house unless it's to go to a doctor, because I always needed a bathroom close by. But I plan on overcoming my fear by the end of the year so I can help others know it is possible."* I did overcome this fear and do attend events and meetings without fear. I just move forward and think to myself I am helping others by what I do so there is no time to worry.

I have accomplished a lot since that day in 2014. I am proud of myself and want you to know you can be proud of yourself too. "I've fallen, cried, have been angry and afraid, but even when I was hurting, I always found a way to keep going. A Strong

Woman never gives up." WomenWorking.com

For more information on Color Psychology See : http://www.empower-yourself-withcolorpsychology.com/color-turquoise.html

I want to encourage you to keep going no matter what; be willing to plant your seeds, blossom and SHINE!

Having belief in your-self is a big step in blossoming

Some ways you can blossom is to plant your seeds and get back to basics:

~~ Take time for yourself and find something that interests you then follow through with it.

For example:

~~ Make jigsaw puzzles for relaxation

~~ Read self-help and inspirational books, then implement what you learned

Work with the color turquoise:

~~ Wear turquoise jewelry or carry turquoise gemstones in your pocket

~~ Write positive affirmations on turquoise color paper and post them prominently

It can be as simple as "I AM HAPPY" or "I AM CALM"

~~ You can plant your flower seeds in turquoise pots to brighten a room and cheer you up

~~ Try to get out into the sun for at least 10 minutes a day

About the Author

Catherine M Laub is a Radio Show Host, Author, Speaker, Psychic Medium, and a Spiritual Guide & Consultant; a Wife, Mother, and Grandmother. She is an 8-time bestselling author and continues her writing in upcoming anthologies. These stories are about her healing and spiritual journeys.

Catherine speaks about mental illness in her campaign "Brighten Your Day with Turquoise", where she shares her own journey with mental illness and a suicide attempt. Here she guides others to feel invigorated and empowered to go forward in their own struggles. She believes you can do anything if you put your mind to it.

Catherine's message is that you are not alone and there is a support system waiting for you. Spiritual Destinations is Catherine's radio podcast brought to you by both the Daily Success Network and RHGTV Network. She interviews people about their spirituality and business ventures. Discussions are not limited to spirituality, because Catherine loves to help others and shares modalities to guide them to feeling better.

Catherine psychically delivers information to people from the spiritual realm, their guides and angels that benefit them greatly with their lives. She compassionately guides them to decipher their lives and plan their destinies. Catherine is a workshop facilitator and does readings at local events, as well as performing sessions with clients world-wide.

Catherine's goal is to open a spiritual store that will also cater to those people who are stressed and need a place to get away for a while. This will be like a mini day retreat, with activities for relaxation. She will do readings in the back along with rent out space for other healers of Reiki, etc.

Workshops and classes will be offered in various categories of spirituality and healing. Her favorite pastimes are making jigsaw puzzles and playing bingo with her mother at local bingo halls. Whenever she gets the chance she travels for vacation and business. The rest of her time is spent with her husband Tony, 7 children and 15 grandchildren. Joshua is her closest because he loves to visit and play with Gama.

catherinemlaub@gmail.com
631-619-2040
www.catherinemlaub.com
Facebook page(s)
https://www.facebook.com/catherine.laub.54
https://www.facebook.com/CatherinesCelestialSpoon
LinkedIn Page:
https://www.linkedin.com/in/catherinemlaub
Twitter handle:

https://twitter.com/cathysquests
YouTube Channel: clmrsavl@gmail.com
Amazon Author Page:
http://www.amazon.com//e/B014M7GZA0
Instagram:

http://www.instagram.com/catherinemlaub

BE HEART-STRONG
By Deb Dutcher

Author, "Sexy, Lean and Strong After 50! – How I went from Fat, Depressed and Divorced to the Best Shape of My

Life and How YOU Can Too!"

Being "Heart-Strong" means many things to me. One is to be strong when tragedy strikes. Two is to create a strong and healthy body, with a strong and powerful heart. Three, help others whose hearts are breaking. Four, stay strong when your beliefs and values are attacked or challenged. Five, stand up for what you believe even when it is not the norm or popular opinion.

Often when tragedy strikes, our heart breaks. Our resolve to stay healthy goes out the window. Our breaking heart is crying out for comfort. We reach for that comfort food – ice cream, cookies, bread, wine, cheese, chocolate. We try to fill the hole in our heart and the missing love in our lives, with food. We ignore the fact that our body needs us to stay strong. We bury the guilt about what that comfort food is doing to our heart and all our organs, not to mention our butts and dress size.

My Year of Loss – divorce after 30 years, followed by the death of my son just before his 20th birthday, then losing my job, home and retirement, all plunged me into a deep depression and longing that could not be assuaged. I turned to food for comfort – usually a pint of Ben 'n Jerry's Cherry Garcia ice cream, followed by whatever cookies or chips were in the house. Over the course of a few months, I ballooned from a Size 6 to 12. I was approaching size 14 when I decided "enough is enough".

Creating a strong and healthy body became my goal. Adding back-in exercise took a monumental effort. Luckily, I had a dog. He needed daily exercise, so we started running in the mornings. Then, I would do strengthening exercises in the afternoon, push-ups, sit-ups, crunches and lunges, and swim. I was able to curb the cravings with good food and vitamins.

If I craved something, I found a way to distract myself. Sometimes I spent a good hour just playing with makeup or outfits. Anything to keep my hands busy and not full of food! Watching TV just triggered empty hands and cravings, so I would put on music and dance the way I used to in high school – all crazy, just moving fast and doing silly stuff, until I would pant and sweat and the only food I wanted was some meat and vegetables.

I went on horse-back riding lessons and took up the violin again. (I was terrible at both, but, I could not eat while doing either one!) I also made sure I hung out with other people who did not binge or overeat. Not necessarily "skinny", but fit and trim. People who would not urge me to "just take one bite" of a cake or pie, when I knew it would end with not one, but two pieces.

Along the way, I started dating and learned that, even at 51, life is not over. Just because my best-friend and lover of over 30 years has decided I am no longer the love of his life, I do not have to roll-over, dry-up and eat candy! I am sexy and viable and I *matter* and someone will love me! It is a very difficult transition, from thirty-year wife to dating. Many of my clients are dealing with it, and it can create real stress. But, it is also exciting and rewarding and fun to meet new people. I met a new love, we married and now live in a town outside the bustling Bay Area. We are in a rural area, with a slower pace. A few years after the divorce, while I was rebuilding my life, body and heart, I became a nutrition coach, and looked for others to help. **It took my mind off my own troubles and I could focus on what would help them.**

My old life as an engineering Vice President was behind me; I got really serious and started studying nutrition. I certified with several groups: Sanoviv Medical Institute, American Fitness Professionals Association, Institute for Integrative Nutrition. I would study nutrition and fitness for hours a day. I learned that, even though the common thought is "you can eat anything in moderation", that is not true for everyone. If you are dealing with illness or obesity, you should not eat just anything in moderation. First, because moderation is somewhat subjective. Two cookies is now moderate for me, but for some of my clients, it would be four or five. Second, because the tiniest amount of something bad for your body is BAD for Your Body.

If you are dealing with an illness or a lot of excess weight, it is just going to exacerbate the problem by causing your body pain inside (inflammation). You won't even know it is bad for you until your body sends you a signal – headache, indigestion, bloating, skin irritation, constipation or diarrhea. How do you figure out what is bad for your body? You become a "mad scientist". You can do an Elimination Diet (see www.sexyleanandstrong.com for the how-to's) to remove all potential problem foods, then add them back in one at a time and really pay attention to what your body says. It is all about listening to your body and making sure you are not putting it on the "Mad-Body Mountain". I coined that term and use it to help my clients understand what is happening to their bodies – the Mad-Body Syndrome – that is created with toxic foods, toxic thoughts, toxic people and lack of exercise.

Your toxic and unhealthy food could be something deemed healthy, like citrus. It could be the nightshades (tomatoes, eggplant, potatoes). It could be tree nuts. In my case, it is: gluten, corn, dairy, sugar, citrus and the nightshades. All the things I used to binge on! We are raised on certain foods. Our parents grew up with those foods and now, they are part of our life. Many of my Hispanic clients think they are addicted to tortillas and tortilla chips, and they "cannot live without them!" But, as soon as they can cut-back, even eliminate them for a few weeks, the pounds drop-off. Thinking you have to eat something just because you always have is totally mistaken.

As we age, our bodies lose enzymes and hormones. We cannot process, digest and assimilate as well as we used to. But, we keep eating what we always have and start getting a sick body. Our bodies thicken, our middles expand, our energy drops and our brain is not as sharp. If we take up a healthier lifestyle, one that pays attention to our body's needs, not our programmed desires, then we can turn this around.

One of my clients, a woman of the same age (62 at the time), came to me with a broken heart and a broken body. At 5'4", she was carrying 196 lbs. She was bowed-over, with aching back and knees. Her husband, twenty years her senior, had been ill with heart problems, and had passed just before Christmas. It was now May, and she was so depressed and had almost no energy. Her diet consisted of coffee for breakfast, a sandwich for lunch and popcorn and wine for dinner. She was on multiple medications. She had not been below 185 lbs. for over fifteen years. Sometimes the broken heart has to heal before the body can be tackled. In her case, she had not let herself grieve the loss of her husband. She pushed herself through the holidays, then tried to keep their real-estate business going. She had worn herself out, was starving herself, depressed and at her wits' end.

Tackling the broken body, with the broken heart, means learning what that heart can bear. How ready is the person to take on their life and rebuild? In her case, she was able to embrace all the guidance and achieved a weight of 141 lbs. over eight months! She is dating a great guy, super happy and super active. She has kept the weight off for over two years, and follows all the guidelines for diet, exercise and self-care we put together.

Over the years, I have had to defend my process and commitment to healthy living. Many feel it is too strict or boring. But, is it too strict when, at 65, I never need medicine, never get sick, never feel exhausted? Is it too boring to wake up full of energy, power through the day, help many others, and look and feel the way I did in my 30s? It is all about your priorities, and the strength of your heart and resolve. **Don't fall into the trap of feeling you are too old or too sick. The body is a wonderful machine and capable of anything with the right fuel, desire and roadmap.**

Being Heart-Strong is being willing to take back your health, at any age! It is being willing to acknowledge that something has to change, and then making that change. It is not hiding away, continuing to munch on your best friends, the chips and ice cream. It is hard, but it is not impossible. It does not matter how old you are, or what your current condition is. Once you have the desire and your heart is resolved, you can do this!

For a few weeks after the 2016 United States Presidential Election, everything fell apart. I did not sleep, eat right or exercise. I wept and worried. My heart was broken and shattered. I felt such desolation and fear. Over time, by allowing myself to feel and recognize I was grieving, I have recovered. You may be feeling things are just too hard and it will take too long. I urge you to listen to your heart and give a new way of being a real chance.

Just ask yourself, "What would make me happiest, right now?" Is it: more energy, less weight, more free time, more love, more money, more family time. What is it that you feel you are really missing? How can you create it for yourself, right now? Just decide and focus on that for the next 30 days. Things that seem too hard just need us to make a heart commitment, set our goals and **Not Be Swayed.**

Here are some tips to follow to identify what you want, how to set some goals around it, and how to stay focused when times get hard:

- Set aside time to visualize what you want your life to be five years, one year, six months from now. Write a paragraph (or several), describing who you are, who

- you are with, what you are doing and how you feel and look. Really feel yourself in each situation!

- Based on those visions, identify a few things you can change in the next six months. Determine what steps you will need to take. Break it down incrementally, working backwards. Here is a goal from a client: "I want to go to Disneyland with my grandchildren in the Fall, and not be exhausted". So, I need to start by: Losing weight, getting some daily exercise and building up my stamina.

- Then, it is about building a plan that gets you to that goal, posting it somewhere you will see it daily, and making sure every night you review it, congratulate yourself on moving forward and stay focused on your goal. Get help from a coach if need be, but stay on track!

- Finally, **Love Yourself,** first and foremost. Who you are today and the Who you are Becoming.

Be Heart-Strong and Reach All You Desire!

About the Author

Deb Dutcher is often referred to as the "Energizer Bunny". She founded her company, Energy Unlimited Coach, to help people have unlimited energy in a safe and healthy manner. At 65, Deb is in the best shape of her life. She is determined to help others reach their optimal condition as well.

Deb has been working in the nutrition field for over fourteen years, and certified as an Integrative Health Coach through the Institute for Integrative Nutrition. As a Corporate Wellness Consultant, she works with executives and their teams to create high-functioning, health-conscious employees, who know how to incorporate healthy activities into every day. As an Executive Health Coach, she has helped high-powered individuals uncover what is making their bodies mad, developed individualized programs to reverse it, and helped them get leaner and stronger.

Her career includes management positions at many of the top companies in Silicon Valley – including Applied Materials, Synopsys, Inc. and Deloitte and Touché Consulting. Deb knows how it feels to be a stressed and overweight executive and entrepreneur and how to get you back into top condition, with systems and programs that fit into your schedule and lifestyle.

Deb coaches her high-powered clients to make themselves and their health a top priority. Her mission is to help others avoid the pain and loss that she had to go through. She teaches them to tune into what their bodies are saying, to feel when their body is mad and to make the changes necessary to get back to sexy, lean and strong. Deb focuses on the whole person – mind, spirit and body. By age 50, most people give up on themselves, figuring they will "just be fat/old/sick". Deb teaches it is never too late.

In her best-selling book, "Sexy, Lean and Strong After 50!", Deb shares how she found herself overworked, stressed, depressed, out-of-shape and at the end of a 30-year marriage at age 51. After losing everything -- marriage, home, and her 19-year old son -- she pulled herself out of the depths of despair to being the healthiest and happiest she has ever been.

In her book, Deb discusses how life challenges, such as depression, divorce and aging impact our emotions and chemistry, which can lead to, what Deb calls, "Mad-Body Syndrome". Deb gives you a road-map to get off the "MadBody Mountain" and back to the "Sexy, Lean and Strong Valley". She provides simple and effective fitness, nutrition and self-care strategies that help folks reclaim their natural vitality.

Deb feels age is just relative. It is all about how strong your heart is, what you are willing to take on, and how hard you will work to reclaim your vitality. It is never too late to get "sexy, lean and strong!"

Email: deb@energyunlimited.biz
Phone: (650) 400-2612
Website: www.sexyleanandstrong.com
Facebook: www.facebook.com/sexyleanandstrong and www.facebook.com/energyunlimitedcoach
LinkedIn: www.linkedin.com/in/debdutcher/
YouTube Channel: Sexy Lean and Strong -- http://bit.ly/1ScwzZm

MIRROR MIRROR
By Jon Missall

When I look into a mirror in the mornings I always thank the mentors in my life that directed me to this point in time. I need to mention them briefly as they have led me down this past and the first one is the infamous Walter Cronkite who at young age took the time to listen to my radio tape and give me not only advice but encouragement to follow a path in media. The next is Len K. who mentored me as I climbed the corporate ladder at Time Inc. for ten years and always kept me on the right road to reaching my dreams in and out of media for many years after my departure.

The last was a woman named Sheila who kept me driven but always believed I could accomplish whatever I wanted as long as my passion stayed true. There are several others but these three really set the tone and I hope that by passing on some of the advice below that in some small way it will help you reach your goals knowing there will be pitfalls and highly rewarding successes along the way.

I am really not the type of person to open up about all the downfalls or successes that I have had but I will say that in over forty-five years of the media, business and the music industry that the greatest reward is seeing others listening and applying some of the ideas below that fit their road to success and watching them succeed.

Passion, Goals, Desire, Accountability and Patience are all the keys to growing a seed into a full blossomed plant of your dreams. Hopefully the following thoughts will help you to reach beyond your expectations and achieve whatever you desire in life so let's start now.

Define your passion and believe in it every day when you awake and think about it before you end your day. Once you have defined what your passion is and have fully committed to it, it is imperative that you map out a strategy to get there knowing that there will be bumps along the way. The important part of passion is that it isn't what is in the moment, it is what you honestly believe is that intangible that will drive you to success. How do you define it? Are you willing to take advice, listen to others, be honest with yourself and are adaptable enough to change course when needed and if the answer is yes to all of the above then you are ready to move forward to success as the seed it planted?

Let's now discuss goals and their various parts. It is imperative that you have short, medium and long term goals that are realistic and attainable. Short term goals should be in a time frame of inception to a three to four-month period with bi-monthly reviews of progress. Put a focus group together of a couple each of respected friends, colleagues and people not associated with your passion. Set your sights for your goal steps twenty percent higher than what you would like your results to be and should you have any setbacks you will still be on schedule to accomplish what you would like along with staying on your growth pattern.

Medium term goals do not have to wait on any time frame of your short-term goals, if you are ahead of schedule, move forward as you are fertilizing the plant properly and growing and beginning to bloom. This should be roughly your six months to a year time frame. Are you still passionate about what you are doing? Don't be afraid to answer those questions. Try not to get to far ahead of schedule regardless of progress unless you are fully equipped to handle that rapid growth while still paying attention to what has brought you success to this point. This stage of your success should lay your ground work for the long term and is extremely important so as not to lose your perspective for your longterm success and humbleness. It is now that it is also imperative that you listen to those around you that have helped you get this far and choose your decisions wisely. Don't underwater or overwater as your successes start to mount.

Long term goals are not the end game but should be your way to fulfilling your passion for as long as your dreams remain the same or you blend them with others which means your path to success has begun to really bloom with branches sprouting to other opportunities that will let you expand. Keep the prize in sight and remember to keep your path going forward regardless of any small bumps in the road.

Desire should be feeling along with passion that drives you each and every day. Do you believe in every aspect of what you are doing and is your sincerity coming across to everyone you touch? Desire and passion are two factors that no one can fake. It is you, your thoughts, the way you live your life and your integrity. People you touch will react to you when these traits come out and will follow you as they realize that their seeds will grow along side of yours.

Accountability is not only about you and your staff but about how you handle it and them. Be honest, thoughtful whether with yourself or others. Evaluate everything carefully before you are too judgmental with others and always speak with them with the dignity and respect that you would expect them to be toward you. Often people in charge are more critical of themselves than others are, so take a step back and listen carefully to yourself. Be honest but don't compromise your values or your goals because you are seeing success and getting to conservative. It is always okay to make mistakes, just handle them in a way that everyone knows you are together to grow towards success.

Patience plays a huge part in your passion becoming a reality. There is very fine line between waiting too long and not moving forward when the time presents itself. Risks are always a part of success but if you wait too long or are distracted by outside influences you will tend to stall. What's the time to move? Go back to your basics and your goals, reevaluate where you are in your plans, the stage of your growth and you will know when the next watering phase is due. Plan carefully at the beginning and your patience will pay off as you continually move forward.

When you have practiced all of the above and can honestly say that you keep all of these in your mind on a daily basis it is now time to watch the fruits of your labor blossom. By this time, you should have also put plans into effect for the branches on your plant so they can follow the steps to bloom on their own as you continue to expand and move forward.

The last step is a daily ritual when you wake and the last thing before you retire for the evening. Look into the mirror and be honest with yourself. In the morning are you ready to go above and beyond to keep the passion alive?

In the evening, can you honestly say you gave everything you could to bloom for what you wanted to achieve for that day? If they answer above isn't always yes, relax and realize how you will get better the next day. Not ever plant or flower blooms at the same rate, but passion, persistence and honestly within yourself will take you farther than most people who will not even get started. LOOK INTO **THE MIRROR AND BE HONEST WITH YOURSELF.** You will succeed! Believe in yourself and others will believe in you.

About the Author

Jon Missall is the Director of TV Programming for VoiceAmerica.tv and a Senior Executive Producer for VoiceAmerica Talk Radio.

With over 35 years' experience in the Business, Music and

Entertainment fields, Jon brings a passion and vision into the VoiceAmerica family that is seldom seen in today's competitive markets. Whether pursuing guests or sponsors for his host's he has been called charming but with a relentless pursuit for perfection towards accomplishing his goals.

For more information please contact Jon directly at 1-4802946419 or email him at jon.missall@voiceamerica.com.

Facebook.com/jmissall
Twitter:@jmissall
Linkedin.com/in/jonmissall

I AM A 'HOLY SHIFTER'
By Beverly Brooke Peterson

Tick tock, tick tock…. watching the clock tick to the upright position of the number 12, and hearing the outside noises, I silently ponder my advancing life... This New Year of 2017 is announcing a true benchmark. Seven and one half decades! It is now TIME…to 'Bloom Where I am Planted and SHINE' In this New Year, the job of unraveling my coincidences and synchronicities has me wondering how I have been able to *Light* up my own life ~ and the lives of others.

I am Beverly 'Brooke' Peterson, an Agent of Change. As a

SeniorPreneur ™ (the new 75 is the old 55!) … I have had lifechanging circumstances, synchronicities and coincidences which have guided me to my **LIGHT.**

I have been inspired, transformed and rejuvenated many times.

Have you experienced coincidences or synchronicities that have moved, delighted, frightened, and/or inspired you too? "A new awakening is occurring in human culture, brought about by a critical mass of individuals experiencing their lives as a Spiritual unfolding, a journey led forward by 'mysterious Coincidences'. (The Celestine Prophecy)."

Many 'coincidences', and 'changes' have appeared in my life, and now, at this 'SAGE AGE' in my 7th decade, I have looked for meaning and found ways to understand them. This is the story of 'My HOLY SHIFT'!

To transform, to BE an Agent of Change, and BE THE CHANGE I WANT TO SEE, seemed to be the reason I was born! Following my Spirit without hesitation, developing my intuition, and learning to co-create a life I am loving to live, has been my path. Being vulnerable, following, understanding and allowing my coincidences and dreams is the journey I have come to experience. Some have called me the 'Black Sheep' of the family. Many of you may resonate with this 'title'. It is quite descriptive. <u>Welcome to the club! Embrace it!</u>

Moving from the left-brain corporate world as a Technical Recruiter and entrepreneur, to becoming a right-brain Holistic Health practitioner, then following my spirit was done by dreams, gut feelings, and learning to follow my intuition.

Do you remember the 5th Dimension singing "The dawn of the Age of Aquarius"? It was a beginning of me

'remembering' what I came to do on planet earth.

On October 5, 1989, I was living in the Santa Cruz mountains during the Loma Prieta 7.5 earthquake. Some lost their lives, and others were 'shaken awake.' The consequence of this breaking of the earth, caused an awareness of the ache and urge in my soul. I *knew* there was **MORE** to my life, and now my internal 'foundation' had been 'moved.

How could I move from left-brain thinking to right-brain woo woo actions? 'Just Follow Your Spirit Without Hesitation' was the answer I received. The *'How'* was NOT going to be easy. We all have 'volunteered' to come to the earth during this time of immense change. And by 1999, I was 'guided' to go to Florida. It seemed to be 'sensible' to take a 3-week course at Hippocrates Health Institute. But Spirit moved, and buying a home in Florida was its plan! ***Had this been my Destiny all along? Had Spirit called me to make these massive Changes?***

I Graduated from Hippocrates with a certification as a Health Educator and Raw Foods educator. This gave me more tools for my transformation box. I was catapulted into Alternative and Holistic Health practices, and I began to create my living as an advocate for Alternative Health practices and Holistic Health products in the direct sales industry.

Starting a new life in 1999, right before the dotcom crash, seemed to be a blessing! While riding the wave of change during the 'crash and burn' of the housing collapse, in 2008, the challenge caused the short-sale of our home by 2012! The loss was devastating! Then moving into a motorhome (mega downsizing), caused more confusing changes.

I had a CHOICE... wallow in being a VICTIM, or, become a VICTOR! Be the Agent of Change! Understand and practice the Laws of the Universe.

An abundance of dreams came inspiring me to move back to California~ here we go again!

Following my Spirit!

Within two WEEKS of driving off from our Florida roots, Bob, (my husband since 1984) was in trouble! He was driving the big rig RV, and towing his car. I was leading the way in my car.

On the night of March 14, 2014, I did not see his headlights anymore. We were driving in the 'Hill Country' of Texas. I called, and surprisingly Bob answered. He had pulled off in the only place that could accommodate a 60' rig! (Angels were watching over him!)- A veterinary hospital circle driveway. (Angels were watching over him!) I called 911! The EMT, Police and Fire Department were just about ¼ mile away. They arrived in just minutes, quickly determining Bob was having a heart attack. (Little known fact, back pain can be a sign of a heart attack!) **Coincidences and miracles were flowing!**

This little town of 3800, not only had an emergency hospital one mile away, but a helicopter waiting to air-lift Bob to the Austin Heart hospital 75 miles away. The cardiac physician said if he had not been air-lifted, he would have died.

Bob's son, Mark was a professional driver from UPS, and had just retired, so he was able to fly to Austin to drive the motorhome to Las Vegas for us. The homeward journey was filled with more miracles, coincidences and each 'dramatic incident' was 'shielded' by angels.

Bob had been in the Army as a young man, and therefore was entitled to Veterans benefits. He had not previously 'signed up' however. Upon arriving in Las Vegas, we headed for the Veterans Hospital. This 'magical' and 'coincidence-filled' experience told me how 'connected to the LIGHT' we really are. Bob was NOT being allowed to come into the 'system' because he did not have his veteran's papers with him.

An angel veteran in a wheelchair magically appeared, who was in charge of the admissions department. This southern angel, (Bobby Dean) assured him that he was there to help his brother Veterans. Within minutes, he retrieved Bob's information (whiz typing on that computer). Bob had remembered his service number. Bobby Dean had us laughing all the time! Another click on the computer, and Bobby Dean had found him! Bob, are you 'Corporal Robert F. Peterson?' Wow! Yes, sir, that's me! So, Bob was admitted into the Veteran's system, and even 'sent' to the emergency room. Bobby Dean said it was to make sure he was treated right away.

The head of the emergency department physicians discovered Bob was having kidney failure! He was quickly admitted to the hospital for several days' stay. She was a GRADUATE from the Hippocrates system, and was surprised that the renal cell carcinoma (kidney cancer) that had plagued him in 2007 had not killed him. She said it was fatal but the tumor was the SAME SIZE now (in 2014, as it was when he was diagnosed in 2007) . . . (My work with holistic nutrition and alkalized, restructured water had STOPPED the growth of the tumor). This doctor added the use of this hydration system to his prescriptions. Coincidences continued to flow in our lives, and after only two more months, Bob was permitted to travel to California for my granddaughter's college graduation.

Another incident occurred that was life-changing. We were with my family on May 18, 2014 in California and Bob awakened with a stroke. (Spirit knew where we were supposed to be, at the time we were supposed to be there!) What a CRAZY way to have us STAY in California! My dreams had manifested!

By this time, one year later, both miracles and scary things were happening. Bob was doing much better (he had learned to walk and talk again), but our motorhome and cars were repossessed. One of the most emotionally embarrassing factors: Bankruptcy…Bob was not formally associated or enrolled in the Veterans' system for the first weeks of his emergency treatments. Many thousands of dollars of preVeterans bills were not able to be incorporated into the Veterans system. My Direct Sales business was also failing! Oh No! Living on Social Security was NOT what I had planned on. And, moving back with family has been another **GIFT** and healing miracle.

What's next?

Becoming a Victor, or remaining a Victim? Being up-rooted, and forced to live in the **LIGHT** was my only way to make sense of all of this! This is **MY HOLY SHIFT!**

My 5th Dimension job ~ my Vocation of Destiny ~ is upon me.

This journey has led me to being a speaker and guide for transformation.

I am honored to help others navigate their murky waters of change.

To support you on your journey, Spirit spoke to me in an acronym: L.I.G.H.T, which means: L.iving I.n G.ratitude, H.armony & T.rust. I created a 30-day mastermind and journaling process to change your frequency, to help you with your Holy Shift!

Welcome to the L.I.G.H.T!

L.iving I.n G.ratitude, H.armony & T.rust

Spirit has been speaking to me in Acronyms – My way to define the word

ac·ro·nym (Definition from Webster's dictionary):

'A word formed by combining the initial letters of a multipart name, such as NATO from North Atlantic Treaty Organization or by combining the initial letters or parts of a series of words, such as radar from radio detecting and ranging'.

This is my 'Divine Interpretation' of the acronym called:

L.I.G.H.T' "L.iving I.n G.ratitude, H.armony & T.rust."

The Divine Qualities of this acronym of **L.I.G.H.T**, flowed effortlessly. It made the meaning easier and more conscious for me to understand that I am a LightWorker.

'*Living In Gratitude, Harmony & Trust' is what is bringing me through this journey.*

Ask yourself these four questions...One for each beginning letter:

L.iving **I.**n. How are you **LIVING**, and being immersed **I.**n this day?

Being immersed IN something so much different than just existing.

G.ratitude

If you are ***Living 'I.n G.ratitude'***, WHAT SHOWS UP for you? (Our vibration raises when we focus on gratitude, and we change our point of attraction! Good things are ***ALWAYS*** waiting for us!)

H.*armony*

What does ***H.***armony FEEL like in your daily world?

Harmony impacts what you SEE and HEAR out there, like on social media, etc.? Did you know that you can react or create? You are ALWAYS a co-creator of your experience. BTW: React and Create have all of the same letters. THEY ARE JUST ARRANGED DIFFERENTLY. This is the process we too can use.

JUST ARRANGING things DIFFERENTLY ~ in our minds'-eye! …. And what about ***T.*** **T.***rust*

Good grief! Do ANY OF US KNOW WHAT'S GOING TO HAPPEN NEXT? NO! If we <u>cannot</u> **TRUST** the Universe, it can be quite a scary life! But, when we are ***LIVING IN TRUST***, we can <u>feel</u> safe, connected, supported & co-creative!

A BIG Plus is BEING in AWE of the way life unfolds! Your Invocation of the Divine qualities of ***L.I.G.H.T.*** therefore can:

Clarify confusion and doubt * Help find a way though mental/emotional overwhelm

Heal feelings of anger, fear, sadness, unworthiness and shame * Help attract resources * Bring guidance as to your next step

When you make a resolution to 'discover' what invoking the Divinity of **L.I.G.H.T**. means to you, your focus and vibration will be raised up. Write in a Gratitude journal for the next 30 days. Become the conscious co-creator of your Divine TRANSFORMATION and REJUVENATION. As you FEEL into the words, you can write your OWN definitions!

Create a NEW ***H.A.B.I.T… (H.aving A.wesome B.rilliant***

I.deas T.oday!)

I hope this story, and my tools for transformation support you on your journey. I might have been 'displaced', 'discouraged', tested and 'confused.' But, I always 'Looked for the Good and praised it!'

If I had not been ***Living in Gratitude, Harmony & Trust***, I may not have followed my Spirit without hesitation, nor stepped into my 5th Dimensional work or Vocation of Destiny. My gifts are many. I have found this Community and group of powerful authors. I am ever grateful for Rebecca and the coincidences of our meeting. I am ready to Bloom where I am planted….And SHINE! Back 'home' in California…

*I am 'Lady Rejuvenator, your **TRANSFORMATION** AND*

REJUVENATION Guide

May you step towards your powerful transformation, and rejuvenation! Bloom and SHINE! – no matter where you are Planted!

These are the times of massive change which we all volunteered to be born into. I call it the **HOLY SHIFT!** Many are suffering needlessly. It is Brooke's pleasure to support transformation, rejuvenation and vitality. It is never too late to rejuvenate and Re-create your life!

About the Author

Beverly 'Brooke' Peterson, known as Lady Rejuvenator, is a 'SeniorPreneur ™' who is half-way through her 7th decade. As an Agent of Change, **'Lady Rejuvenator'** inspires Transformation, Rejuvenation and Vitality. Brooke is an advocate for Ageless Living Solutions.

She has a varied background, with over two decades in the corporate world as a technical recruiter and business owner in Silicon Valley.

Did you know that one of the biggest hiring issues is that disease causes work-related absences, and lack of project completion? Brooke's soul called her to 'be the solution'. With an on-going asthmatic condition, herself, researching alternative medical solutions was a natural and important process.

Years of study led her to find her passion in alternative, drugfree and spiritual healing methods. Brooke even received a certification as a Health Educator at Hippocrates Health Institute in West Palm Beach, Florida, where she learned what Hippocrates said, 'Let your food be your medicine, and your medicine be your food'.

She is also a successful Direct Sales entrepreneur focusing on health-related products. Her husband Bob was given a dire health verdict. It was reversed with the use of her alternative products! She has 'many tools in her tool bag', and with advancing technology, she embraces state-of-the-art, drugfree solutions. She is your **HOLY SHIFTer!**

561-628-1845

BeverlyBrooke44@gmail.com New science of Age Reversal: www.Brooke.hGHbreakthrough.com
www.LadyRejuvenator.com

www.BBrookePeterson.com

Section 5
SHINE!

*We all have the ability to **SHINE!** Gain tips, tools and insights to help you discover how to share the gift of you with those around you...making a difference one heart, one connection at a time. Be willing to show up fully in your life and **SHINE** the gift of who we are with the world.*

CONFIDENCE—THE ART OF BEING CONFIDENT
Have the Confidence to SHINE
By John F. Hall, LCDR, USN(Ret) MBA, BSEE, MSCS

I have often been asked how I came to be confident. People have wondered about my journey to becoming confident and have asked "What is your secret?" In response, I will share what I know.

Feeling Confident versus *Acting* Confident.

Merriam-Webster defines the word "Confident" as "having or showing assurance and self-reliance." I have often wondered, which comes first... *feeling* confident so that we can *do* things with confidence, or *doing* things confidently so that we can *feel* confident? You know, I haven't always been confident. My confidence level was essentially non-existent as a teen.

When I was in high school we were a rather poor family consisting of my single mother and her three wonderful (?) children. As a single mom, she was raising us while at the same time finding time to study for her college degree.

Having very little money, we wore the cheapest clothes owned, inferior bikes, and generally carried only the very least expensive basic school supplies. I didn't join the tennis team because of my embarrassing "K-Mart Special" tennis racquet. These items were always scrutinized by unforgiving classmates. This merciless mocking for having inferior things negatively impacted my feeling of self-confidence. I became shy and introverted. All I wanted to do was to be invisible and just graduate.

Upon graduating from high school, I joined the Navy. I entered boot camp carrying my duffel bag and my history of being insecure, shy, and introverted. One of the purposes of boot camp is to break down the individual only to build back confidence through discipline, "instruction", and seemingly endless drills. However, after completing the 13-week grueling "confidence-building" ordeal, I didn't *feel* any more confident after boot camp than I did before boot camp. I *felt* that I was the same shy and introverted person as before. The problem was that my new uniform (not to mention my new "buzz" haircut) would not allow me to remain low-profile, and I stood out even more.

But suddenly I was treated differently by my peers! What changed? (Certainly it was not my **feeling** of having no confidence.) I was the same unconfident person, but people treated me more respectfully than they had in high school. Now when I walked into a coffee shop, my peers talked to me with a sense of respect. It seemed that my *actions* had created a new reality of a confident person! I had the positive prop of a uniform to help me *act* differently, even though I *felt* the same lack of confidence I had felt before.

I gradually came to embrace the rising feelings of confidence stemming from the confident *actions* I was unwittingly taking. **The *action* of confidence was leading to the *feeling* of confidence!**

A similar thing happened later in my career the day I was promoted from being an enlisted person to receiving a Navy Officer's commission. One day I was sitting on the bus "swapping sea stories" with my fellow enlisted sailors, yet on the next day after receiving my commission they were now rendering crisp salutes and addressing me as "**Sir**"! I was the same person on one day, but the next day I was treated with much more respect and appreciation. I was now wearing the Shoulder Boards of a Navy Officer. **The *action* of putting on those Shoulder Boards rather than any *feeling* of confidence is what made the difference!**

"Wear your Shoulder Boards"

I discovered that if you want to be more confident and are not sure how to break the cycle of having to *feel* confident before *acting* confident or *acting* confident before *feeling* confident, I would suggest that you **take an *action*!** I found that it is much easier to control your actions (particularly with a prop) than it is to control your feelings.

Actions don't care how you *feel*, so if we can take an *action of confidence* (wearing imaginary Shoulder Boards), we are not only appearing confident, but our *feelings* of confidence will grow!

Think of someone who you believe is a very confident person and observe **their** "Shoulder Boards" ...that is... how they move, talk, and interact in ways that cause you to *believe* that they are the model of confidence. If that person walks into a room with their head held high, speaks in a steady voice, and looks around the room as if they were the owner of the venue rather than a guest, then attempt to mimic their *actions*.

Attempt to mimic wearing **their** "Shoulder Boards" and be sure to let people see them!

Don't be afraid to show them prominently. The bolder you "display" them; the easier it is to hide behind the "Shoulder Boards" and their actions, and the less need to rely on a *feeling* to generate confidence. Don't you feel more drawn to the person who reaches out to take your hand and give you a warm smile? People will respond to the *actions*...they will react to the "Shoulder Boards".

Practice at home first using a mirror and their "borrowed Shoulder Boards". Display them proudly. Notice your posture and be sure your shoulders are back and your head erect to get the full effect. Visualize entering a room full of people you've never met. Walk around with your healthy posture, reaching out to shake a hand and introduce yourself. Always *act* like you belong and people are interested in meeting and talking with you. ***Feel*** those imaginary Shoulder Boards... and trust them…they soon will be your own. Practice that action in the real world, and you'll notice a sense of accomplishment which will boost your *feeling* of confidence. **But the actions can come first, *before* the feelings!**

"There is no try; there is only Do and Not Do"

Yoda, Jedi Knight from Star Wars movies

When Master Jedi Knight Yoda was told by younger Jedi Knight Trainees that they would "try" to use his methods to tap into the "Force" to save the galaxy, his response was absolute. He declared that there is no "Try". There is only "Do" and "Not Do".

Have you ever *tried* to get to the bus stop on time in the morning? You may try skipping breakfast, dressing faster, getting up earlier, etc. but with all of that trying, if you still are not at the bus stop at 7:15, the bus still leaves and you will have missed it. Trying is *not* a result; it is only an effort and an attitude. There is certainly nothing wrong with trying hard (trying hard is commendable) but the result of any effort can be evaluated in terms of measuring whether the goal was accomplished. Each time you will be measured for a *result* of "Do" or "Not Do", and if the result is "Not Do", then you simply try again until you achieve the desired result.

Gaining confidence can be a hard thing to do. That, however doesn't mean that it can't be done, it just means that it is exactly that…*hard*. Each misstep is a learning experience toward gaining confidence, and each learning experience creates a new confidence level that can be eventually lead to success, or" Do". The result will be "Not Do" until it is finally "DO" and then you are there!

The eye cannot say to the hand, "I don't need you, or the head to the feet, "I don't need you"

-----1st Corinthians 12: 21-22, Intl STD Version

Another aid to building confidence is to remember our life's purpose. As indicated in the Bible verse above, **I believe that we each have our own special purpose in life. I believe that not only do we merely have a purpose, but it is indeed our <u>responsibility</u> to fulfill our specific purpose.** The purpose of the whole body of society may be larger than the individual. I may be only a "hand", or an "eye", but the "whole" depends upon **me** to complete **my specific** function and purpose. . I need to ***truly shine*** as the "eye" or "foot". This truth has helped me to muster the strength to take *actions* to *become* confident, knowing that it is my responsibility to fulfill my purpose, and therefore I ***must*** do it.

Sometimes our specific purpose may not be clear. Family, careers, environment, or health sometimes may thrust us into unfamiliar or difficult situations. Therefore, we can find ourselves planted in places where our purpose is difficult or uncomfortable…. but that often is when the growing and blooming is most important for completing our specific purpose. Not much growing needs to take place if we always seek out places (or a purpose) where we are comfortable.

We must carry out our responsibility to best of our capability, and indeed shine for the purpose and place in which we find ourselves. This belief has helped me move to a level of confidence by using not only my props of "shoulder boards" and "confident acting", but also the sense of responsibility for my purpose.

Promise me, you will always remember: you're braver than you believe, and stronger than you seem, and smarter than you think" ---Christopher Robin to Winnie the

Pooh, as written by A.A. Milne

These words inspire me. They remind me that we **can** do things that we may not *believe* we can. They also remind me that we **can** successfully mimic the actions of confidence if we practice it.

How many times do we hold back from doing something because we don't think we can do it, or simply because we have never done it before? When did accomplishing something new translate to "can't do"? **Just because we *think* we can't do something, or have never done something before, does <u>not</u> mean we can't actually do it!**

We are much more capable than we may think.

Have you ever tried to convince someone that they could do something even if **they** don't believe they can? I remember when my daughter was learning to ride a bike. The bike had the training wheels and we had been periodically raising them as she became more comfortable with riding. There was the day when I was pushing her and she was afraid that I would let go and she would fall. Now **I knew** without a doubt that she could ride that bike without the props, or training wheels.

Well, as you can imagine, I ran along beside my daughter on the bike as she shouted "don't let go, don't let go!", but the thing is, I had **already** let go and she was riding on her own. She was able to take the *actions* of confidence even before she *felt* confident. She was much "braver than she believed". You may have heard nightmare stories from returning prisoners of war as to the condition and inhumane treatment they had to endure while being held captive. These were conditions that no one would think they could possibly endure, yet these brave people did. They were braver than they believed...as are each of us.

We can endure much more than we believe, and we are much stronger than we seem. So, believe in your highest self, but know that you are capable of even much more...you are smarter, and now more confident, than whatever you think you are!

Take *Action*, the *Feeling* will Follow

So, if you want to be more confident, I would suggest that you put on your "Shoulder Boards" and *act* like they are firmly in place on your shoulders. Start taking the *actions* that those shoulder boards command! Know your purpose and responsibility. And either "DO" or "NOT DO", but keep working until the result is "DO"!

And just like with my daughter, I **KNOW** you can do it. You are braver that you believe. Now think about that…you believe a certain thing about yourself, but **no matter what you really believe, you are even braver yet…braver than you think you are!**

Final tips to help you "Put on Your Shoulder Boards" and increase confidence:

- Don't worry about *feeling* confident…try *acting* like someone who is confident (but practice with their "Shoulder Boards" first!). The *feeling* of confidence will follow.

- No matter how unconfident you **think** you are and what you believe, **KNOW and BELIEVE that you ARE more confident than you feel. You are braver, stronger, and smarter than you know.**

- Take on the purpose that is dictated by where you are planted with a renewed sense of responsibility (and perhaps urgency). Do this to your utmost capability.

These steps will help you sense those imaginary Shoulder Boards on your shoulder, take action, and you will surely **Bloom Where You Are Planted and SHINE!**

About the Author

John Hall has a servant's heart.

He was born in Kentucky and spent much of his childhood helping on his grandparents' farm in southern Ohio. There he learned a lot about the interaction of humans and nature, and to serve at the mercy of the uncontrollable events of nature.

The crops were dependent on nature, and sometimes nature didn't always cooperate (or more truthfully, the other way around). His serving continued when he enlisted in the Navy to serve his country. He was promoted through the enlisted ranks and earned a commission as a Naval Officer and retired from this era of serving others as a Lieutenant Commander. He earned a Bachelor of Science Degree in electrical engineering from the University of Washington, a Master of Business Administration (MBA) from John F. Kennedy University, and a Master of Science degree in Computer Science from The Navy Postgraduate School.

Today, John is a successful business owner and entrepreneur who draws upon his vast life experience of serving others to mentor people who are looking for independence. John fiercely believes in personal independence and he helps people improve their lives to become less dependent on others for their wellbeing.

sailor180@hotmail.com
(707) 372-8282

MY MOSCOW ADVENTURES
By Barbara Gross

As the saying goes, by Ralph Waldo Emerson, "Life is a journey, not a destination."

I believe in every situation; we have a choice to laugh or cry and I choose to laugh.

Some people ask me, "Why do all these funny things happen to you?"

I reply, "If you listen carefully, they may not have been so funny at the time!" It's all in how you look at things. Do you choose to see the humor in unexpected things as a challenge and an adventure? How do you tend to see things? In thinking about our perspective and choosing to embrace the adventure, and to find the humor in things, My Moscow Adventures still come to my mind and heart. Can I share with you some stories and experiences that I had lots of opportunities to choose my response?

Five years ago, I was interviewing for a position as a Business Development Manager for a Computer Software Company.

Initially, I interviewed at the local headquarters based in Northern California but ultimately I was going to report to a woman at our International Headquarters based in Moscow. So, once the US Office decided I was a good candidate for this position; I had a couple of Skype Calls with who would be my manager in Moscow and it was decided that I would be hired.

Once I was able to get all of my papers in order for a Visa, I was to fly to Moscow to meet everyone I would be working with in person. As the procedure goes, I needed to give my passport to a 3rd party company to generate and complete all of the paperwork for this Visa. My flights were arranged to travel to Moscow in March as to give enough time for this paperwork to be completed and I was supposed to receive my passport, as well as, receive a new Visa, before my flight.

When the package did not arrive at my office as scheduled, I called customer service to see if they could track the package. I gave them all the details & they told me that a supervisor would contact me within the hour. Needless to say, I never received a return phone call, even though they were informed that the package included by passport & that I had a flight the next day. I then started calling every hour to track the status of this package. It seemed that no one from this Overnight Mail Service was taking any kind of ownership of this issue to even give me a courtesy phone call, to at least let me know, that someone was looking for this package. I would also like to emphasize that this particular document was MY PASSPORT WITH A RUSSIAN VISA.

In order for me to expedite getting a new passport, I ended up going directly to the San Francisco Passport Office. When you have had, unexpected things happen and delays?

How do you choose to respond? Does your attitude become negative, do you get frustrated and stressed? Or are you able to find humor in the situation and enjoy the journey, and unexpected turns? I think it's important to stop and check in on these things so that we are actively choosing who and how we want to be in the world no matter what happens to us.

My perseverance paid off and I did eventually make it to Moscow a month later. But this was just the beginning of my adventures in Moscow. (In looking back, perhaps these VISA challenges and delays were a timely reminder that things don't always go according to our plans.) Two years ago, I was asked if after our corporate meeting, I would like to attend a party.

Well, my middle name is 'party' and of course I signed up!

As I said, I signed up for a party but I didn't receive the agenda until weeks later and my airfare was already paid for, so there was no turning back. However, instead of just your average party, this event turned out to be an extreme sports adventure.

The agenda is as follows:

- Hiking up and down a mountainous river bed.
- Zip lining over a forest.
- Mountain climbing & rappelling.
- Diving into a river.

As I read about these activities, I started to get a little nervous as I am not the kind of person that would sign up for these kinds of activities. In fact, I don't even own a backpack. Even though everyone at my company can speak English, I can't speak Russian! So, if I got stuck in the middle of the zip line, I might still be there; but I had committed and when I commit to something, I do it. But let me tell you, this agenda was completely out of my comfort zone. Have you ever been faced with something like this? Where you thought, you signed up for something fun and familiar only to discover their definition of a 'party' is very different from your own. What do you do in those moments? I discovered, I bring the party with me in how I show up, choose to laugh and embrace the adventure.

In addition, how we got to this campsite area was to take a 2hour bus ride from Moscow to the airport, to take a 2-hour plane ride, to then take another 2-hour bus ride & then be loaded on a truck that looked like it came from World War II.

The only way I could get on the truck was to be pulled up by fellow colleagues as there were no steps and as they were pulling me up, they shouted to me to watch my head as I was getting in for fear I might just smack my forehead.

Also, I guess I was not paying attention to all of the items I needed to bring in order to survive in this wilderness, for instance:

- A light to wear on my head as there were no lights at the campsite. This was especially important when finding the outhouse. Oh, yes, the outhouse. There was no shower or toilet, just a hole in a very small hut (I can't even begin to explain the smell)!!! I also neglected to bring my own toilet paper as the campsite didn't provide any so I was constantly begging if someone could "spare a square".

- I did not bring a bathing suit & it turned out to be 100 degrees with 100% humidity. So, the coolest thing I had to wear were the clothes on my back that I left with from the USA. Long black leggings & a baseball shirt. During the 1st event of hiking up & down a mountainous river bed, I was sweating so much, I looked like I had been in the water only I hadn't, until we came to a waterfall & I just bent over & dunked my head in the water. Everyone was so proud of me that I had finally experienced the waters of Russia, I usually don't wear sneakers. For anyone that knows me, I either wear flip-flops or heels as I love freedom of feet. My brother does not believe I even own a pair of sneakers just to give you an indication of how athletic I am. However, sneakers were mandatory for this adventure. During the course of the hike, the rubber from the bottom of my sneakers started to separate & flip off so they had to have a guy cut off the rubber bottoms with his pocket knife.
- They recommended bringing a backpack. Somehow I missed that and brought my beautiful clutch purse to carry my things in throughout the adventure. I kept trying to keep the clutch tucked under my arm (as it didn't have handles) and eventually someone offered to carry it in their backpack.

Needless to say, after the 1st event, I decided to be the onsite photographer & let the others enjoy their sporting experience, while I participate in a 'bonding only experience' with the whole team. I found a way to participate and connect that was a little bit more in line with playing to my strengths in connecting, bonding, and building community and relationships and let them have their athletic adventures.

I got to take this whole bonding thing to a whole new level as I shared a tent with 2 other co-workers. We were given sleeping bags to lie on the ground in our tent & I was in the middle. You just could not help to get to know one another better. I never took my one & only outfit off for the whole weekend as it was the coolest thing I could wear because the extra stuff I packed was long sleeved as there was a possibility it could get very cold at night and it never did. However, even through my pants, the mosquitos were after me. When I say that every square inch of my body was bitten, I am not exaggerating. The only part of my body that was spared was my face and I think the reason for that was that once the mosquito got close to my head, I could wave it off as I could hear them coming from the buzz in my ear.

The evenings were a lot of fun as we sat around the campfire singing songs for hours but I would just like to say again, I just signed up for a party!

If you learn anything from what I have just shared with you, go ahead, sign up for a party but make sure you see the agenda 1st and go with the flow and have A Great Time no matter what! In fact, be the party and bring the party with you.

The following year, my company was having another annual business meeting in Moscow for a team building event. **This year I was going to be prepared!**

I purchased clothes that had bug spray, extra bug spray, hats and even a net to put over my head! For fun, I actually wore the same outfit from the previous trip (the black leggings and baseball shirt) to joke around with them. I wanted to get a laugh when I stepped off the plane wearing the same outfit

I had worn the entire 'party trip' letting them know I was ready.

However, this is what happened; again, things didn't quite go according to my plans. It turns out the joke may have actually been on me and not the other way around.

I always try to get to the airport in plenty of time to check my bag & go through security. This trip, I arrived to the San Francisco Airport in plenty of time, however, there is a very long line to check my bag.

In addition, because this was an International Flight, I was told by my company that I could check my bag at a Domestic Airline in San Francisco and they would then transfer my bag to the International Airline directly to Moscow.

I rushed to the gate in San Francisco to find out that my flight was delayed for a half hour and to make matters worse, once I landed, I had to sit on the tarmac for another half hour.

It turns out that Los Angeles to Moscow Flight was delayed due to baggage problems. So, my colleague held a place for me in line and I was able to board the flight in time.

But, sadly, even though the Domestic Airline took my bag to check it through to Moscow, **they did not deliver on their promise.** What do you do when you count on someone or an organization and they don't come through as promised? How do you choose to respond? I found out later that it had been sitting at the San Francisco Airport for 2 days before they discovered that they needed to put it on the next International Flight to Moscow.

I would receive emails from the International Airline that the bag had arrived in Moscow, but when I called to see when they could deliver it to my hotel; they could not manage to find it? I was wearing the same clothes for the whole time I was in Moscow about ten days. This started to feel very familiar, despite my careful planning.

I had four days of business meetings and four days of jeeping, horseback riding, motorcycling and team bonding exercises in the forest (sometimes in mud and sometimes in pouring rain) so my boss generously shared her own sneakers, socks, sweater and raincoat. All in all, as each day passed, I just thought it was funnier and funnier!

My bag finally arrived the day before I was about to leave for the USA, just in time to make the return trip home with me. All of the special clothing I purchased for the trip (even though very wrinkled) still had all of the sales tags on as I was never able to wear them so the retail store let me return everything without question. They even let me return all of the bug spray and suntan lotion even though the boxes were totally smashed!

Really, I was prepared this time, I read the agenda.

Remember:

YOU can't always control what happens to you, But YOU have control as to how YOU would react in any situation. Here are my tips to help you choose to be joyful, to bloom and shine bringing that joy-full light and life to any given situation:

Choose to be positive

Choose to help others as they have helped
Choose to give people the benefit of the doubt
Choose to have the courage to be our authentic selves
CHOOSE TO LOVE.

How About YOU! What do you choose? How are you choosing to be in the world? **Barbara's Bonus 'Party' Tips:**

Read the Agenda

Follow the Checklist of Supplies

Be open to how the party/life/event flows (and look for the fun, and celebration and story) Remember to laugh and Bring the Party! (Your love, light, joy, humor, and laughter.)

About the Author

I was born in Massachusetts and after graduating college became a native Californian, however, my accent will have to be surgically removed.

My degree is in Education & I have been a teacher but I am currently a Business Development Manager for Computer software and have been in the Software industry since 1990. Bachelor of Science in Education from the University of Massachusetts in Amherst, MA President's Club

Awards for Sales & Technical Expertise from Xerox Imaging Systems/ScanSoft and Vice

President of Membership at ' ABBYY Talk ' Toastmasters Club in Milpitas, CA for, 4 years.

I would like to express my love for life by showing people how being able to laugh at oneself is great fun!

When people meet me, they ask me, "Why do all of these funny things happen to you?" and I reply, "If you listen carefully, they were not so funny, at the time!"

I have learned that being my authentic self is what I want to be and show others why that is valuable, as I have proven this to myself and others with the success I have achieved in life.

I think I have a story about almost any topic but below are some of my topics from my YouTube Videos: https://www.youtube.com/channel/UCTe05eh2e8D8-PLCOz-EFyw

Baaaaahston	My Boston Accent
Horseback Riding	Horseback Riding Stories
Embarrassing	No Water, Drying Cleaning & Visiting College
High Maintenance	Discuss Why I Am "The Director Of High Maintenance Women
Pachos	Taking My Dog To The Veterinarian
Traveling	Mishaps While Traveling
Birthday Shirts	Funny Birthday Party

blgross@sbcglobal.net (650) 575-4636
https://www.facebook.com/barbara.gross.9047
https://www.facebook.com/baaaaahbra/"
https://www.linkedin.com/in/barbaralgross
https://www.youtube.com/channel/UCTe05eh2e8D8PLCOz- EFyw

THE WORLD IS MADE OF STORIES
By Caitrìona Reed

I am driving south through a green landscape, sun soaked after days of torrential rain. The air is so fresh and clear. I feel that I could reach out and touch the distant mountains. I am coming home from the mastermind meeting that I've been attending every month for the past year-and-a-half. Each time I go it feels like another kind of home-coming. I meet with a dozen women; successful business owners, all of them deliciously down-to-earth in their wisdom, openness, and strength. I am in awe at my good fortune in finding a place for myself among them, my new family. **I celebrate what it tells me about the person I have now become.**

When I first requested to join the group, I didn't hear back for a while. The director later told me that she had to do some soul-searching about whether it would be appropriate for me to be part of this group, because, as I say these days when I introduce myself publicly, "My name is Caitrìona, and I am a woman of transgendered experience."

Going about my everyday life, I can easily forget that a statement like that, a *story* like that, can challenge

others to reflect on what it means to be a woman or a man. Transgender visibility may have increased exponentially in the last few years. But it seems that many people are still uneasy when they come face-to-face with someone who has actually made that journey. They are challenged to examine some of their deepest assumptions. "Is she a *real* woman? Is he a *real* man" What *is* a *real* woman?" "Am *I* a *real* woman, or man, or business person, or artist, or parent etc." or whatever identity happens to be up for question. The question might even arise, "If someone can change their sex, what else is it possible to change?

I grew up as a boy child. Despite years of hesitation, and a couple of false starts, now and for the past twenty years I have moved through the world as a woman. I do not flinch. I have let go of the shame and doubt that haunted me for so long. I no longer ask myself whether I am a **real** woman.

My public introduction usually continues, "I am a woman of transgendered experience, and I've learned a whole lot about big scary changes, and committed decisions."

The leader of the mastermind has become a good friend, and even told me that she has learned something from me about what it means to be a woman. It's the bit about scary changes and committed decisions. After all, don't we all have to make those at some time in our lives, no matter who we are?

Sad as it may sound, my own big question was, not whether I was a *real* woman or a man, but whether I was a *real* human-being?" My bewildered sense of gender identity forced me to wonder if I even qualified as a person.

Other people seemed so self-assured, so certain of their boyhood or girlhood. I longed to put an end to the turmoil of my endless questioning, and the shame that fed it. "Why couldn't I be like my grandmother, or my mother, or my friend Carolyn?" The little boy inside me had to find another question. He needed to find a place to rest.

If life is made up of stories, I had to find a new story to tell myself, and to tell the world. If life is made of stories, then we owe it to ourselves to make it a really good story, one that serves us well, and that might even help the people around us too.

Most people have made up stories that feed old regrets, or their guilt, or excuses for why their life has gone a certain way. All such stories, in fact, are true, because we make them into self-fulfilling prophecies. And all stories serve a purpose, although that purpose may be to just keep us locked into a familiar place, because familiarity is safe. William James suggested that, "truth is what is useful." **What if we committed to a story whose usefulness was that it declared, with full voice, that we can be strong enough, joyful enough, and creative enough, to show the world, and everyone in it, how magical and beautiful and powerful we are?**

Twenty years ago, feeling not in the least bit, magical, or powerful, or beautiful, I made my public announcement to the world and came out of the proverbial closet. Actually, I had already had my foot half way out the door for some time, but I still couldn't make sense of it. On the one hand, it felt like a non-issue. What's a little gender-bending after all? What's so scary about a bit of androgynous self-expression? On the other hand, I feared, with good reason, that changing your sex can make a big dent in your life, financially, professionally, socially, and in lots of other ways.

It can alienate the people you love. It also demands that you become seriously self-obsessed, at least for a while. So, I had an operation to become a middle-aged virgin. In the process my psyche had to perform a series of fast-forwards and rapid rewinds to reinvent itself. I had to re-vision my childhood, puberty, and coming of age in my new gender role. I had to make a new story. It was not a deception, not a rewriting of history. It involved creating a new internal landscape that demanded, above all, that I just accepter myself as I was, as I had always been.

You've probably heard the metaphor about a woman being trapped in a man's body. It is a convenient story to explain the transsexual experience, but it's way too small. I felt that my whole spirit, the essence of who I was, was being stifled. **Something inside me was clawing at the walls for release. I was ready to burst open. It didn't even feel that it was to be about gender at all. It was about something much more fundamental to who I was.**

So, I took a leap of faith, a leap of necessity. In large part, it was my partner, Michele, who pushed me. We were Buddhist teachers. We were leading meditation retreats around the U.S., in Europe and at our center in Southern California. For years, we had been teaching the art of being present, the joyful skill of bearing witness to the exquisite fabric of living in this very moment, integrating the world of activism and social responsibility with spiritual practice. Around that time, I had been changing the emphasis of my teaching, and talking about the importance of being authentic, of being truly embodied. Also, much of the work I was doing with my clients at that time had the same focus. People were coming to me less with symptoms, and more with deep existential questions, trying to get a handle on the central meaning and purpose of their life. **It's astonishing how accurately the world reflects back to us the lessons we most need to learn ourselves!**

Then Michele gave me the ultimatum. "We can't go on like this. You've got to make a change one way or the other. I can't stay with you unless you do. If you're going to change your sex - just do it!" So now I can say, "My partner made me do it!" But the reality was, and remains, that as artists, and as teachers, we made a transition together, and the transition continues. Stories never end.

Our work as a human being is never done. The priority is to be true to what calls you to show up in the world as you are. **Unless you are true to your story, and find ways to keep it resounding with meanings that are real for you, then you are on the slippery slope to becoming a robot, and living by someone else's story.**

Some of the stories that infuse our collective consciousness are so insidious. *"You are broken and need to be fixed." "Nothing you do can make a difference." "Someone or something outside of you exists that will save you."* What if we changed that? What if you committed to a new story? A story that let you bloom and shine, here and now, right where you are? You are a living system, co-creating yourself in every moment. You are interconnected to a larger living-system we call life, the universe, creation, or by any other name. The universe is fundamentally safe. **You are not broken. Everything you can imagine is possible.**

Your story is your own. Mine is my own. My story demands that I remain true to myself, that I am visible, that I accept all of who I am, that I affirm my humanity, that I continue to transform fear and uncertainty, shame, and regret. I've learned to shine not as someone who happens to have changed my sex, but as an artist of change. I embody the entirety of who I am, so that the work I do, to help others change and bloom and shine, is free of any expectation of what that's supposed to look like. Your story is yours to tend to, like a flower coming into bloom. Know that the very things you thought were keeping you from blooming may turn out to be the source of your greatest power and strength. **Let your new story evolve and grow as a shining reflection of who you are.**

A home-play exercise to support you. There's an exercise we learned many years ago that we still use in our workshops and with our clients. It works well if you are at a point in your life where you feel stuck, or at a time when you need to make a big change, in your work, relationship, lifestyle, your relationship to money, to your own health, to anything. It involves writing and journaling, and most importantly, it involves finding forty minute to an hour when you won't be disturbed.

Begin by sitting quietly, and taking a few breaths. Tune in to whatever it is that is causing you to want to make a change. Tune in to wherever in your body you sense disquiet, uncertainty, fear, or regret. Allow yourself to feel it. It doesn't have to be a strong feeling. If you feel dullness or numbness, then tune in to that. Being aware of the feeling is just a way to set the scene.

Now begin to write a list of some of the elements in your life where you have felt victimized, discredited, blocked, overlooked, unseen, or helpless. Write without selfcensoring. Just write. You don't need to write out the full story. Just jot down a word or phrase that conveys the memory and feeling of that time. Write it all. Assume that it all matters.

Take your time.

When you have finished, sit for a moment and tune into your body and your feelings again. Maybe you'll discover that there's more to write. Keep going.

Then when you feel you're finished, take a break. Stand up. Shake out the tension.

Next you're going to re-write the story of your life as a Hero's Journey, or a Heroine's journey, or as a journey of yourself as a superhero. You'll start at the beginning. You can begin with, "Once upon a time," or, "A long time ago, in a galaxy far away." Think of the fairy stories you heard as a child, or of the mythical journeys that are at the center of all people of all times. Think of the resources and strengths that you developed through all the challenges and setbacks. Remember that you are a survivor, you made it. Here you are. **Create a new story that places you on the brink of brilliant exploits and adventures.**

Keep writing. Take the story into the future. Imagine all you can achieve. Imagine the positive impact you can continue to have. Expand it exponentially. What would you take on if you knew you couldn't fail? Dream it! Write it as large as you like.

When I opened to the truth of who I am, I was afraid that my life, my career, even my credibility as a human being in society, was in doubt. Now life continually reminds me that I am whole. The work I do with my clients continually affirms that I am living my true story, and that its truth can touch the lives of others in ways more powerful than I could have ever imagined. I encourage you to create your heroic journey showing you thriving! May you bloom and shine your beautiful light fully into the world.

About the Author

Caitrìona Reed has led trainings, workshops, and retreats worldwide. Her listing in Wikipedia names her as, "An American Zen Teacher in the lineage of Thich Nhat Hanh who has dedicated her life to integrating authentic spiritual training with engagement in the 'real' world."

She currently mentors successful business owners, artists, and creative entrepreneurs to embody the magic of their soul's masterpiece and be seen, and to **be**, in the world as the visionary they are. *"When we dance at the dangerous edge of our creativity we step into the life we imagine, and help everyone move closer towards the world we long for."*

She also is co-founder and co-director of Manzanita Village Retreat where, with her partner Michele Benzamin-Miki, she holds trainings and retreats. Her work is a synergy of ancient sacred practices with applied brain science, and socially engaged spiritual practice.

Originally from England, Caitrìona is a woman of transgendered experience. She notes, "I finally learned that you owe it to yourself, and to everyone, to become fully and authentically visible. If you are to step into your role as an evolutionary leader and co-create the world that we are longing for, you must first become aligned with the truth of your own soul."

www.fivechanges.com
https://www.linkedin.com/in/caitrionareed/
https://www.facebook.com/caitrionareed
https://twitter.com/CaitrionaReed

BLOSSOM IN THE MIDST OF THE STORM
By Trisha Garrett

I returned home from a trip to Southern California last night and as I sit and reflect on my travel experience, I am given insight that I would not have recognized in the past. I am surprised at my responses and how much I am changing. I am blooming and shining in places that are unexpected.

I realized to bloom where you are planted and shine is a state of being and not something that you do. To bloom where you are planted becomes a way of life. It is a lesson that God has been teaching me the last several years and I didn't realize it until now as I am writing this chapter. You can be anywhere, dealing with difficult circumstances and how you decide to react or respond is important because it determines how you show up in the world, impacting those around you. You bloom and shine when you relax into what is, accepting it and allowing "it" to teach you so that you can show up in a powerful way positively impacting those around you. You can bloom in the midst of the turbulence.

I recently traveled from where I live in Northern CA to

Southern CA to participate in a three-city transformational event for young girls and visit my family. The morning started out wonderful as I had pack the night before and I was all set. I was looking forward to the trip. My plan is to arrive early into Burbank, while it was still day light and then drive to San Diego and spend all afternoon with family. It has been several months since we hung out and this makes our time together that much more special. I glance at the clock; it is time to head for the airport. I gather my purse and luggage and make my way to the front of my building. I pull up the app for the car service and it is not working correctly. The app loads and opens but I am not able to navigate the app. I try for several minutes only to notice that time is starting to slip away. Let me try one more time. I am starting to get nervous and I can feel the tension starting to grow in my body. So, I shut down the app and reboot my phone just to make sure everything is running correctly.

Oh, no, maybe that was not such a good idea, my phone is rebooting at a snail's pace. I glance at my watch and I am running out of time. If I don't leave in the next 15 minutes I could miss my flight. I have cut it close before and I still made my flight. I can feel myself starting to stress. I take a deep breath and I tell myself that this time will be no different. It will be fine. *(Have you ever been in a situation where time was slipping away from you and you are trying to figure out how to regain control as your stress level rises and frustration sets in)?* Ahh the reboot is complete. Ok, it's going to come together. I open the app again and same problem. Now I am starting to get frustrated, which does not help. I choose to remain calm and look at my options. I can drive my car? No, the time it will take to park my car and catch the shuttle, I will miss my flight. Maybe I should use another car service? That means I will have to download the app? I feel like that is the best option. I was able download the app with no issues and request a car.

Yes! The car service will be here within five minutes. The 5 minutes turn into 10 minutes. I look at my watch and it is now 20 minutes later. Now I am worried and feeling helpless, it's not looking good. I am nervous I don't think I am going to make my flight, however, I choose to remain hopeful. In the mist of all of that I called the airline only to be put in line for a call back. I was intentionally trying to avoid Los Angeles Airport because it is so big and congested and traffic is a nightmare 80% of the time; Burbank Airport on the other hand is small and it feels manageable. I am bumping up against the time and I will soon be late for my flight. Finally, the airlines is calling me back. Although undesired, if I miss my flight I can fly into of Los Angeles since there's flights almost every hour. The airline agent confirms that I will miss my flight. Disappointed, I remain calm and discuss my options. The best solution is to fly into Los Angeles. Burbank's next flight is not until late afternoon. Bummer!

I arrive safely in Los Angeles and at baggage claim waiting for my bag. I hear on the loud speaker my bags will be on carousel 2, 15 minutes later, it's carousel 1. It's now 30 minutes later and no bags. Another announcement, my bags will be on carousel 2. Another announcement, apologizing and letting us know that our bags will be on carousel 1. It is now over an hour later and still no bags. Finally, my bags appear on carousel 2. I scurry out to catch the shuttle to the car rental location. I see my shuttle and I rush to cross the street. Just as I make it over to the platform my shuttle drives off. What? No way!! The day is becoming an adventure and now I am wondering what's going to happen next. I sit and relax because it is going to be another 15 minutes before the next shuttle. What started out as a simple trip, 1 hour flight is turning into a crazy day of travel. It's now raining.

I am approaching the car rental entrance as the rain is pouring down. Entering the building, I can see the line is wrapped around a couple of times. I smile and with acceptance for what is and say to myself "looks like I am going to be here awhile. Forty-five minutes later it is my turn. I approach the counter and the gentleman asked, "Ma'am, do you have a reservation?" I respond, yes and provide my name. I sigh with relief and gratitude as he confirms my reservation. He looks at me and says, "I am sorry but we have no more cars in your class I think to myself, of course not, and I wonder, is there a bigger purpose to all of this craziness?

Nothing has gone according to plan and I continue to relax into what is. It is becoming clear to me that by going with the flow; with what is right now, there's a calming I experience. I am able to genuinely smile at the agent and with a gentle tone to discuss options. Ten minutes later he has a car for me. It is still pouring down rain as I run out to the car and put my bags in the trunk. I get in and ready to drive off and the car is small and has no amenities. One big wind and I would be blown off the freeway. I go back and by this time I am soaked from the rain and ask if I could please have a mid-size car that I requested.

He goes to the back office and returns with a smile on his face. A car was returned so I just had to wait 15-20 minutes for the service department to clean it up. I was going nowhere fast so I said great! What else was I going to do?

Thirty minutes later I have my new set of keys and I am off to San Diego. There have been so many unexpected events today. It has truly been a crazy travel day and it is not over. All day I have had to pause and accept what is.

Have you had a crazy day where you have to remember to pause, breath...accept what is...acknowledging the things that are out of your control. Remembering that you are always at choice to react or respond? With a smile on my face I found myself constantly saying, "this is crazy" to the point where it became hilarious.

By this time, it is 4:30 pm, it is dark and grey skies and I am dead center of the storm as I enter the freeway. Still soaking wet, I turn on the heater and it works!! I am excited. The wind is blowing as the rain is coming down so fast I can barely see. Alert...flash flood warning goes off on the GPS. Yea, thanks for the reminder. I take a deep breath and remain calm....and notice...that something is shifting in the atmosphere.

As I drive down the highway, each car was consciously driving to keep themselves and their passengers as well as everyone else on the freeway safe. It felt as though we were all in unison slowing down to 40 miles an hour or less as the rain came pouring down almost to the point of blinding us. We were connected on this crazy travel day; each driver choosing to be in support of one another in our respective journeys to get safely to our destinations. I sit up straight in my seat. Eyes open wide looking ahead and intensely aware of the cars on the side and behind me.

An alarm goes off on my phone reminding me that I am in the midst of a flash flood. As the rain is plunging down, I hold tightly to the steering wheel, I observe that the other cars were making sure that they maintained a safe speed. Each car kept a reasonable distance in front and behind them, just in case an unforeseen surprise happen. I noticed cars approaching on my left, I instantly felt my body tighten up preparing for the big blinding impact of the splash across my windshield, but it never happened.

With all that has gone "wrong" I was expecting the worst. I have to remind myself to stay open to new possibilities. As the drivers approached my car they would slow down drastically minimizing the impact of the splash to my windshield. This was amazing. I have never had this experience before where it appeared that everyone was in consideration of the next driver. While driving through the storm, there was a peace and a calm even though I remained present with all senses on alert. This peace was like an amazing energy surrounding me and the car. Although my hands were firmly grasping the steering wheel, it felt as though this energy was controlling the car and clearing the path before me; allowing me to rest even deeper in the calm of the peace.

In the mist of the storm I realize I was setup to be right where I was at in that moment, in the midst of the storm experiencing an overwhelming sense of peace, feeling safe and held by something far greater than myself, the Holy Spirit.

Strangely enough, I am in the middle of a storm and I am feeling safe…I notice the calmness of my response. It's a strange feeling because I realize it is still very important for me to continue to be present and drive defensively with everything around me. In the center of the storm there was a calming as the cars flowed together down the freeway.

At the end of my crazy travel day full of unexpected twists and turns I realized that I had actually experienced a major shift in what I was choosing for myself to be present. Not putting any energy on the things that I could not control. Accepting what was before me and resting in it and remembering to stay open to new possibilities. In each situation throughout the day I had chosen to bloom where I was planted. I had choice even in the craziness and the unexpected. Perhaps this unexpected crazy travel day had actually been a day full of opportunities for me to choose to blossom and shine. To smile, be present, flexible, and choose to be empowered instead of frustrated and stressed.

Summary:

Each time I let go of my concern with time, it seems to allow a natural flow or movement. With each exhale of breath, and a releasing of frustration, tension and stress there's a forward of movement of intangible things making way for them to manifest in the natural realm. I give myself permission to reset if necessary and embrace the opportunities to bloom and blossom.

To blossom where I am planted has begun to take on a deeper and much powerful meaning for me. **I** have discovered that just like when a flower blossoms, it is beautiful, when I blossom, I am beautiful. For many years, I struggled with my self-image so it is empowering to know that to blossom, to be beautiful has nothing to do with the physical appearance. It has everything to do with how I respond to life's challenges. To be calm in the midst of a storm.

To celebrate what is working (like when the heater in the car was actually working). How I am being and what I am choosing from moment-to-moment. To be present, recognize and embrace the sweetness that is happening around me is new and empowering. To be in integrity with my values and not wavering. I bloom, shine and I am beautiful.

Here's tips to help you embrace the unexpected and step into your beautiful blossoming self:

1. Being/Present/Awareness

- When things start feeling out of control, stop, take 3-5 deep breaths and ask yourself what is really important to me now? How do I want to show up in my world based on my values?

2. Release Control and expectations

- Let go of the check list or any expectations or things that you felt were a "must". Rest into what is…see what is available to you now.

3. Acceptance

- This can be a time of giving yourself permission. Permission to accept what is or what isn't, releasing it and being at peace, a time of joyful acknowledgement.

4. Learning

- As you are being present with what is, also be curious and ask "what is the learning?" Perhaps it is learning to be present with what is. It can also mean you are simply aware that an opportunity to choose is available to you.

  To reflect and acknowledge with no judgement if there's any shifts or if things have remained the same.

5. Choose Gratitude

- No matter what our circumstance, whether we are celebrating or having a crazy day there is always something to give thanks for, to be grateful.

About the Author

Trisha is the Owner and Executive Producer of BriteLiteTV Channel which is on the recently launched RHGTV Network. BriteLite TV Programming reinforces that You Matter, You are Enough and You are Powerful through; Inspiration, Education and Personal Empowerment. Trisha is the Host of the "Trisha Garrett Show".

Articulating her creative flair "Trimiah Presents…" was created to bring diverse expressions of entertainment; Both shows are syndicated on VoiceAmericaTV.com.

Trisha is an International Amazon Best-Selling Co-Author *(Come Out of Hiding and Shine)*. Trisha's a frequent guest on Talk Radio shows and Panelist for Speaker Talent Search where opportunities for the candidates to be seen, heard and expand their audience.

Core to her passion, for the 20 years of Trisha working for Fortune 100 Companies in Silicon Valley several of those years she managed Girl's Technology Day at Intel Corporation. The event introduced, simulated, and encouraged over 100 girls each year from underserved communities interest in (STEM) careers.

A drive and on purpose to help women stand up, live bigger, and thrive deepened as she volunteered with a non-profit organization, which helped women to assimilate into mainstream society. Trisha headed up the mentoring and coaching program while providing educational, career and life coaching for single mothers.

Trisha is a certified life coach that provides programs that encourage collaboration. She is building a community that empowers women to stand in their greatness to bring change to communities and illumination around the globe.

www.britelitetv.com

www.facebook.com/britelitetv
www.twitter.com/britelitetv
www.instagram.com/britelitetv

CLOSING THOUGHTS

I hope you have been touched by the powerful stories in this book and have been encouraged on your journey of blooming where you are planted and SHINE! We can't wait to see you, hear from you, and celebrate you as you share the gift of you with the world!

We want to thank the amazing authors who shared their transformational stories and messages. We also thank WOM Enterprises for embracing our vision for this book and helping us share it with the world. I want to thank my husband for always cheering me on and encouraging me to SHINE! God, thank you for giving me opportunities, opening doors, and bringing together the right people for this powerful project. I thank my parents for their love and support and my grandmothers for planting the seeds to Bloom Where You Are Planted and SHINE!

****

We wanted to share about some additional books Rebecca is part of and some upcoming books that you may also enjoy that we are excited to be publishing.

Books compiled or written by Rebecca Hall Gruyter to be released in late 2017 or 2018:

The Grandmother Legacies, this anthology features over 15 grandmother legacy stories and was inspired by Rebecca's Grandmother Stories. Rebecca discovered as she shared her stories, many men and women also had powerful stories of their grandmothers. These heirloom stories share how powerful women have impacted our lives and created an enduring legacy in our lives that we are bringing forward in our lives and businesses. This uplifting book shares powerful and precious legacy stories with the world. May the voices, sharing the legacies and wisdom of our grandmothers live on, touching and transforming lives for many generations to come. (To be released in late November/early December 2017.)

Rebecca will be releasing her book titled **"Voices of My Grandmothers, a Legacy from a Granddaughter's Heart** in honor of her grandmothers in 2018. These stories are the way Rebecca started her speaking, writing, and radio career – by sharing about her grandmothers. We encourage you to watch for it as we believe their wisdom, heart, and stories will encourage and inspire you on your journey in life.

Step Forward and SHINE! This anthology featuring over 20 authors (the third book in the SHINE series) will empower readers to discover the actions they can take to move forward and SHINE in the areas that matter most to them. The world needs you NOW! (To be released in August/September of 2018).

BOOKS FEATURING REBECCA HALL GRUYTER

TO BE RELEASED IN 2017:

"The Power of Our Voices, Sharing Our Story" Anthology, compiled by Teresa Hawley-Howard (December of 2017)

Previously Released and available on Amazon *(a book compiled by Rebecca or featuring a chapter or foreword written by Rebecca Hall Gruyter):*

"Becoming Outrageously Successful" Anthology compiled by Dr.

Anita Jackson

"Catch Your Star" Anthology published by THRIVE Publishing

"Come Out of Hiding and SHINE!" Anthology compiled by

Rebecca Hall Gruyter

"Discover Your Destiny" Anthology compiled by Denise Joy

Thompson

"I Am Beautiful" Anthology compiled by Teresa Hawley-Howard

"Succeeding Against All Odds" Anthology compiled by

Sandra Yancey

"Unstoppable Woman of Purpose" Anthology and workbook, compiled by Nella Chikwe

"Warrior Women" Anthology compiled by Nichole Peters

"Women on a Mission" Anthology compiled by Teresa Hawley-Howard

"You Are Whole, Perfect, and Complete - Just As You Are" compiled by Carol Plummer and Susan Driscoll

INDEPENDENT REVIEWS

Ms. Lisa Nobles

CEO/Founder of Empowered Women of Faith & Purpose, Inc.

www.ewofp.org

A part of life is going through its extremities and then learning how to overcome them. Circumventing our worst fears, and tackling our greatest challenges can lead to self-renewal and revitalization. Indeed, the authors of "*Bloom Where You Are Planted and SHINE*" demonstrate these concepts.

They share their individual, compelling narratives of adversity, mystery, triumph, and victory! Their stories tell how life transitions can transform people simply in choosing to flourish, choosing to overcome and resisting a need to be a victim. Here, still, hope can bloom! You too can bloom! Even in the most unlikely of circumstances, SHINE!

Ana Fatima Costa, RPR, CSR
Author, Coach, Speaker, Connection Practice Trainer
www.anafatimacosta.com/coaching

In this latest powerful anthology compiled by Rebecca Hall Gruyter, *Bloom Where You are Planted and SHINE*, I can "hear" the voices of each of the 25 co-authors.

I was transported into their lives as they shared their authentic personal stories and encouragement to readers - heartfelt pearls of wisdom such as, *"Redefine the story and remember who you are at your core"* and *"Forgiveness is the choice you make to hurt and suffer less even though you are wounded."* I feel transformed, encouraged and supported. 5 stars!!

Divya Parekh

Business Relationship Advisor

Three times #1 Bestselling Author

www.divyaparekh.com

The book, Bloom Where You Are Planted and Shine is brimming over with insight. The authors have done a great job of taking us through their inspirational voyages navigating challenges of life that will inspire you to heal, hope, and action.

LeaAnn Fuller ~ Fuller Life Coach
Lovingyourfullerlife.com

Rebecca Hall Gruyter and her Co-Authors have really hit home in this great Anthology, Bloom Where You Are Planted and Shine. These powerful women will speak life into you as they share their raw and vulnerable stories. It is so nice to know that you are not alone and these women prove that you can overcome anything.

Rosalyn Kahn
Author & International TEDx Speaker
www.rosalynkahn.com

It was a true honor to be asked write a review for the Bestselling Author and Writer Rebecca Hall Gruyter for her latest book Bloom Where You are Planted and Shine. From the moment, I read the purpose of the book I was instantly connected. We learn immensely from our deepest challenges.

It was as the author shared her own pain of growing up in hiding, I immediately knew why we connected. I too had suffered in the hidden space and was blessed to come out the other side. Thanks for bringing these stories out to inspire others.

Nella Chikwe
Speaker, Author, Publisher, Purpose 2 Profit Strategist
Founder – The Unstoppable Woman Of Purpose Global Movement www.nellachikwe.com

A compelling heart centered anthology of inspired women leaders sharing how they bloomed in the middle of their difficulties and during their life's experiences. No matter the pain, discomfort and uncertainty endured. They felt the fear and did it anyway! They didn't allow their difficult circumstances dictate their destiny to SHINE! The inspiring stories provides a compass to guide the reader to her greatness.

This book will encourage the women reader to love herself, value her worth, embrace her experiences. To dig deep, straighten up her crown, pull back her shoulders, stand up and SHINE bright like a diamond.

Dear Powerful Reader,

Thank you for reading our anthology. I hope it has touched your heart and spirit; encouraging and inspiring you to bloom and SHINE!

I wanted to share a little bit more about our organizations,

Your Purpose Driven Practice™ and RHG Media Productions™. We are passionate about helping others live on purpose and with purpose in their life and business. I hope this book has supported and inspired you to choose to live on purpose, bloom and SHINE!

If you are wanting to reach more people and be part of inspiring and supporting others with your message, your gifts, and the work that you bring to the world; then I wanted to share some opportunities for you to consider.

Each year we compile and produce anthology book projects, produce and publish an international magazine, launch TV shows, facilitate women's empowerment conferences, launch radio and podcast shows, help experts and speakers step into a place of powerful influence to make a global difference. We provide programs and strategies to help you reach more people, and facilitate the Speaker Talent Search (which helps speakers, experts, and influencers connect with more speaking opportunities.) We would love to support you in reaching more people. Please take a moment to learn a little bit more about us at the sites listed below, and then reach out to us for a conversation.

We would love to have you join us as we seek to make a positive global difference.

You can learn more about each of these things are our main website: www.YourPurposeDrivenPractice.com

Enjoy our powerful TV programs:

www.RHGTVNetwork.com

Learn more about the Speaker Talent Search™:

www.SpeakerTalentSearch.com

If you would like to connect with me personally to explore some of our opportunities in upcoming book projects, podcast/radio shows, and/or TV, then here is the link to schedule a time to speak with me directly:

www.MeetWithRebecca.com or you can email me at: Rebecca@YourPuposeDrivenPractice.com

May you always choose to Bloom and SHINE!

Warmly,

Rebecca Hall Gruyter

www.ingramcontent.com/pod-product-compliance
Lightning Source LLC
Chambersburg PA
CBHW071902290426
44110CB00013B/1254